HOW TO ACE THAT
MACROECONOMICS
EXAM

The Ultimate Study Guide

DAVID G FRAZER

Tellwell Talent
www.tellwell.ca

ISBN
978-0-2288-2650-7 (Paperback)
978-0-2288-2651-4 (eBook)

Dedication

I dedicate this book to my deceased mother, Lillian Louise Brown-Frazer, and my loving aunt Maxine Brown.

Acknowledgements: Monica Przyborowski was a contributor to this textbook.

Special thanks to Dr. Patrishka Duncombe for giving me the idea to write a summarized textbook based on my teaching notes. Special thanks to Dr. Ashli Fox and Ben Gray for emotional support and Captain George Evans for his encouragement. Thanks to George Lei, one of my excellent students, who helped with the question/answer sections.

Table of Contents

Testimonials

"Thank you for teaching me the core concepts of the Macroeconomics tests! On this year's Ap examinations I scored a 5! I deeply enjoyed your classes from day one and believe it or not, now I have a passion for economics and I want to dedicate my life to the financial industry –It was a memorable journey, THANK YOU!"

– David Li, AP Economics student

"Mr. Frazer, I want to happily inform you that I scored a 5 on both AP economics exams. I cannot overstate the positive impact your class has had on me and my understanding of economics. In fact, I am seriously considering it as a potential career path for me in the future. Again, thanks a lot!"

– George Lei, AP Economics student

Introduction

No Frills, No Fluff, No Stress! Everything you need to know to get an A on your exam.

Look, economics isn't easy. It takes time, effort, and an interest in the topic to really retain all the information needed to score an A on your exam. I've studied and taught Economics for over 13 years and have fallen in love with Economic Theory. But I have noticed some of my students struggling with certain concepts and dealing with the frustration of carrying gigantic textbooks that over-explain, over-analyze and over-fluff everything.

Why complicate an already difficult topic?

I've spent years digging through economics textbooks, comparing syllabi, analyzing questions on the Macroeconomics exams, and most importantly LISTENING TO MY STUDENTS who were begging for a study guide that could make sense of all the shaky understandings that they were unclear about. I've realized the information my students needed could be relayed at a fraction of the time, by focusing on exactly what matters, and what exactly will be on the test.

This book covers everything you would expect in your first-year Macroeconomics class, in a college or university, your AP exam, and covers more than the average grade 11 or 12 Macroeconomics class.

In a time crunch? This book only takes 60 hours to read. That's potentially two and a half days to read, understand, practice, review and prepare you for any economics exam.

How do you effectively study for the Macroeconomics exam? I have developed a Cheat Sheet created to help you get through the content and totally secure your understanding of all the concepts explained in this book! And guess what? It's absolutely FREE. If you'd like your FREE Cheat Sheet click here right now and get started studying for your Macroeconomics exam!

If you want to self-study effectively, score top marks on your exam and spend more time living life and less time inside studying, start today!

How to Use this Book, to Get the Top Marks that You Want!

- First, download my Cheat Sheet, and my Free Response Question guide on Amazon! This is a guide that condenses Main Points and Key Concepts into a quick summary that will help you to solidify all the information you've learned and provides you with a quick review for the night before your exam. Think of it as the "cliff notes" version of this book.... all the info you need without the commentary. It will save you time and give you peace of mind knowing that you are studying exactly what you need to ace your exam! To get your Cheat Sheet and Free Response Question Guide, download on Amazon today!
- Spend between 40 minutes and 2 hours reading each module and make notes. Any points you do not immediately capture, do a quick online search to get more information, add those points to your notes. This will ensure that there are no gaps in your learning and that all the concepts are properly understood.
- Memorize all key terms per module to ensure that you will be able to recall concepts quickly.
- Memorize all charts per module, especially noting how changes in the chart affect the x and y axes.
- Attempt each practice question.
- A week before the exam, re-read the book, testing your memorization of key terms and chart changes.
- Three days before the exam, re-attempt each practice question. I promise you it's worth it!
- The day before the exam, take 4 hours to read the entire book and download my Cheat Sheet right here. This process works best for those who spend the time following these steps... even if you waited too long to start studying!

There's one last step, EMAIL ME at acethatexam179@gmail.com or leave me a review and tell me how you did! I want to hear from you!

Good Luck Friends,

David

Module 1:

Scarcity

Economics is the social science that studies scarcity and choice. Imagine a world where everyone had equal access to resources and could take as they please. Do you think everyone would be satisfied with their share of the world's resources? Would the resources be shared fairly? How long would they last? Most of the world's resources are finite. Dividing all the resources of the world among its 7.7 billion inhabitants does not mean that everyone would get what they want.

Scarcity is defined as the condition where the limited supply of resources does not meet the wants and needs of consumers. It is the motivation behind economic choices. Resources or factors of production, such as money, labor, commodities, raw materials, and land, are used to produce goods and services such as cars, computers, education, and healthcare services. These factors are scarce, and consumers are forced to make choices.

Scarce resources become valuable because they are limited and often economically valuable. Almost all resources are limited. Because of this, the goods and services produced in the economy are limited as well.

Everything around us is scarce.

Macroeconomics vs Microeconomics

There are main two branches of economics: macroeconomics and microeconomics.

Macroeconomics is the big picture view of the economy. Economic actors are not viewed individually but as groups. For example, when referring to demand - microeconomics may discuss the demand of an individual or a household while macroeconomics is concerned with the demand of whole countries.

Macroeconomics studies the actions of the government, and public policy, money, the foreign exchange market and economic growth.

Module 2:

Opportunity Cost and the Production Possibilities Curve

Economics is all about choices. People have to make economic choices, and it is important to understand what factors affect these choices. Two of these factors are the *opportunity cost* and the *production possibilities curve*.

Opportunity Cost

In economics, a **trade-off** occurs when a choice is made between two economic goods. The opportunity cost is what you lose when you choose one thing over its' alternative. The best alternative to the time used for an hour nap, for example, would be working and earning $15. So, the opportunity cost of a nap is equal to $15.

In a two-alternative choice, the opportunity cost measures the trade-off when choosing one alternative leads to having less of the other alternative. How do you find the opportunity cost when you are producing two goods? Each extra unit of good $X = (Y_2 - Y_1) / (X_1 - X_2)$.

Let's say Canada produces laptops and cellphones:

Laptops X	Cellphones Y
0	20
2	15
4	10
6	5
8	0

The opportunity cost of producing another laptop $= (10-15) \div (2-4) = -5/-2 = 5/2 = 2.5$

If Canada wants to produce one more laptop, it would have to give up 2.5 cellphones. The opportunity cost of producing a cellphone = (6-4)/ (10-5) = 0.40 laptops. If Canada wants to produce another cellphone, it has to give up making 0.40 laptops.

Production Possibilities Curve

The production possibilities curve (PPC) illustrates how production choices are made when the economy is limited to producing only two goods. The PPC shows that total production is limited by the amount of resources available in the economy. The PPC measures the maximum output of two goods using a fixed amount of input at the highest efficiency; in other words the trade-off between two goods—good A and good B.

Figure 2.1 illustrates the PPC. Producing 30 units of good A means producing 0 units of good B. Likewise, 30 units of good B leads to the production of 0 units of good A. However, producing 15 units of good A yields 20 units of good B.

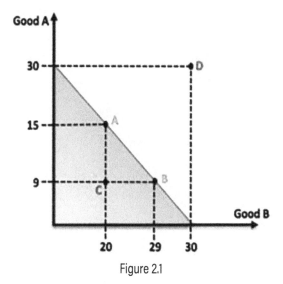

Figure 2.1

The points within, on, or outside the PPC illustrate the feasibility and efficiency of production. In Figure 2.1, points A and B are feasible and efficient; point C is feasible but not efficient, meaning it could easily be produced, but doing so would not maximize output. Point D is efficient but not currently feasible for the economy. In the future if the PPC shifts outward due to technology or productivity improvements, point D may be attainable.

As an economy experiences growth, the PPC continues to shift outward to the right.

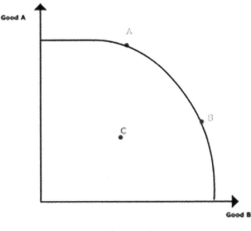

Figure 2.2

The shape of the PPC varies and explains the opportunity cost and production technology. In Figure 2.2, the PPC has a bowed-out curve, which means the opportunity cost of production increases, and goods are different from each other. In Figure 2.1 the PPC is linear, as the opportunity cost of production is constant no matter how much of each good is produced.

Questions

1. Assume the economy produces only two types of goods: military and civilian goods.

Using a correctly labeled PPC, show the effect of an increase in military expenditures labeling the initial point as C and the new point as D.

2. Any point inside a PPC is

    (A) better than points on the PPC.
    (B) allocatively efficient but technologically inefficient.
    (C) associated with inefficient use or unemployment of some resources.
    (D) associated with movement along the PPC.
    (E) associated with constant opportunity costs.

3. If producing each additional unit of good X required giving up ever-increasing amounts of good Y, the PPC between X and Y would be

    (A) bowed outward.
    (B) bowed inward.
    (C) a straight line.
    (D) horizontal.
    (E) upward sloping.

4. Sweden and Norway use equal quantities of resources to produce food and capital goods. The table below shows the maximum possible production of food *or* capital goods for each country.

Country	Food	Capital Goods
Sweden	50	100
Norway	30	120

(i) Draw a correctly labeled graph of the PPC for Sweden. Place food on the horizontal axis and capital goods on the vertical axis. Plot the relevant numerical values on the graph.

(ii) On your graph in part (i), indicate the following.

- A point that represents an efficient level of production, labeled E
- A point that represents an inefficient level of production, labeled I
- A point that represents an unattainable level of production, labeled U

Module 3:
Comparative Advantage and Gains from Trade

Why do companies move their factories to other countries and regions? The answer involves both comparative advantage and gains from trade.

Comparative Advantage

A comparative advantage exists when the opportunity cost of producing a good or service is lower than the opportunity cost if another country produced the same good or service. Every country has a different opportunity cost depending on the countries' natural qualities and resources.

A country's comparative advantage promotes **specialization**, or the focus on the production of goods and services for which a country has a particular comparative advantage. Market economies promote specialization and trade, because doing so is much more efficient and economically productive than having self-sufficient individuals.

Absolute Advantage

When a person, company, or nation has an absolute advantage, it means it can produce a good or service more efficiently than any other party with the same resources. This is important when a nation is deciding which products to put its limited resources into making. For example, if both the United States and China can produce books and mugs, but China can do so at a faster rate, using less resources, for cheaper, then China has an absolute advantage in producing books and mugs.

	Books	Mugs
China	30	90
United States	20	80

6

Here, China has an absolute advantage in books and mugs as it can produce thirty books and ninety mugs, whereas the United States can produce only twenty books and eight mugs.

Gains from Trade

Gains from trade arise when countries benefit from the economic trade of goods based on their specialization. Countries can produce all the goods and services they need and become self-sufficient, but this would often cost much more than importing some goods and outsourcing some services in which they have a comparative disadvantage.

Trade is an important method of obtaining the goods and services consumers need.

Countries are able to raise their standard of living through trade, and it can lead to opportunities that the PPC outward for both countries. Gains from trade in macroeconomics occur when countries increase the output due to specialization and engage in trade with other countries.

David Ricardo asserted that gains from trade contribute to economic growth and cost savings: both from the import of goods from more efficient producers and from the export of goods and services by the country with a comparative advantage.

For a country to benefit from trade, it has to import a good at a lower opportunity cost than it would cost to produce itself. A country can have an absolute advantage but benefit from trade if it has a comparative advantage.

Going back to the example of books and mugs, let's calculate the opportunity costs:

China: Producing 1 book = 90/30 = 3 mugs	Producing 1 mug = 30/90 = 0.33 books
United States: Producing 1 book = 80/20 = 5.3 mugs	Producing 1 mug = 20/80 = 0.18 books

The United States has a lower opportunity cost of producing mugs, as it has to give up only 0.18 books per mug produced, whereas China has to give up 0.33 books, giving the United States a comparative advantage. Therefore, if China specializes in books and the United States in mugs, and they trade, both will experience gains from this mutually beneficial trade agreement.

Questions

1. If two nations specialize according to the law of comparative advantage, then trade with each other, which of the following is true?

    (A) A smaller number of goods would be available in each trading nation.
    (B) Total world production of goods would decrease.
    (C) Everyone within each nation would be better off.
    (D) Each nation would increase its consumption possibilities.
    (E) One nation would gain at the expense of the other.

2. The following table shows the number of donuts or cupcakes that John and Erica can each produce in one day.

	Donuts	Cupcakes
John	200	100
Erica	150	50

    (i)   Who has the absolute advantage in producing donuts? Explain.
    (ii) Who has the comparative advantage in producing donuts? Explain.
    (iii) Assume John and Erica decide to specialize according to their comparative advantages, and one cupcake is exchanged for four donuts.

    - Indicate whether specialization and trade are beneficial to John.
    - Indicate whether specialization and trade are beneficial to Erica.

Module 4:

Demand

Figure 4.1

Demand refers to the relationship between a range of prices and the quantities of goods and services consumers would purchase, as shown in the demand curve Our demand for a good is our desire to buy that good. Demand for a good or service decreases as the price increases.

The **law of diminishing marginal utility** says that as consumption increases, the marginal utility derived from each additional unit declines.

Figure 4.1 illustrates that the demand curve is downward sloping. The demand curve is downward sloping. The quantity demanded in the demand curve shows the actual amount of goods and services consumers are willing to purchase at each price level. In Figure 4.1, at point A, consumers demand 20 units of the product at a price of $20. At point B, consumers demand 29 units at a price of $10.

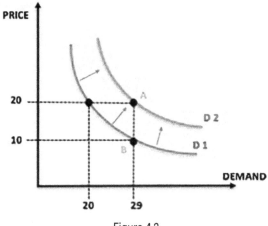

Figure 4.2

A shift in the demand curve happens when a change in a determinant of demand occurs. In Figure 4.2 there is a shift to the right. This means there is an increase in demand at every price level. It is also possible for the demand curve to shift to the left when there is a decrease in demand for a good.

The other half of the market model is the seller's side, or the party that supplies goods and services. **Supply** is defined as a supplier's willingness to produce an amount of goods and services at each price level. Supply may be affected by several external factors of production: land, labor, capital, and enterprise required to make a good or service available to consumers.

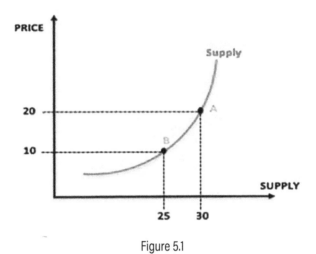

Figure 5.1

What Is Supply?

Supply is a willingness to sell at a given price.

In economics, **supply** refers to the relationship between a range of prices and quantities supplied at those prices. This is reflected in the supply curve. The quantity supplied in a market is the actual amount of goods and services producers are willing to sell at a specific price.

The supply curve in Figure 5.1 is a graphical representation of the supply for a good or service. It is normally upward sloping because producers are more willing to increase the supply of a good or service when the prices are higher. Note this is the opposite of the demand curve.

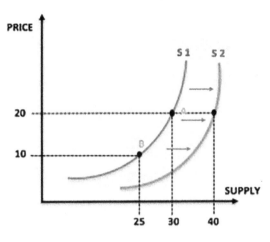

Figure 5.2

The supply of every good is affected by a number of production factors: land, labor, capital, and enterprise. Figure 5.2 illustrates a shift in the supply curve. If the cost of at least one production factor falls, more can be produced, and the supply curve shifts to the right. The factors of production for goods and services dictate the supply of goods and services in the market. Thus, supply is all about incentives to produce goods and services.

Questions

1.   Which of the following is most likely to be caused by an adverse supply shock?

  (A) Structural unemployment
  (B) Frictional unemployment
  (C) Demand-pull inflation
  (D) Cost-push inflation
  (E) Deflation

Module 6:
Market Equilibrium

I like to describe the equilibrium as the sweet spot in the market. Graphically, it is where the demand and supply curves meet; theoretically, it is the price and quantity of a good or service at which all economic actors are satisfied.

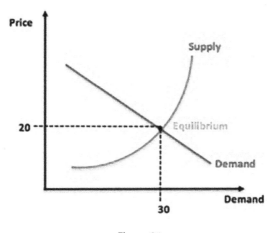

Figure 6.1

You can see this in Figure 6.1 at an equilibrium price of $20 and a quantity of thirty. When this good is priced at $20, no individual buyers want the good at $20 who won't be able to have it, and every supplier who wants to sell at $20 will be able to sell.

Market equilibrium emerges over time after the process of price discovery. It is also known as the market clearing price. The **equilibrium price** is where consumers and producers agree. The **equilibrium quantity** is the quantity at which everything produced is sold to consumers.

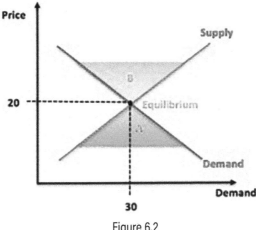

Figure 6.2

Any point above and below the market clearing price signals an inefficiency. In Figure 6.2, section B above equilibrium and section A below equilibrium show this. In section B of Figure 6.2, price points lead to excess supply. At $21, there will be more of this good supplied in the market than there are consumers interested in purchasing it. In contrast, section A shows a supply shortage or a demand surplus. A demand surplus or excess demand occurs when the demand for a good or service is much more than the supply. This happens when the price is set below equilibrium.

When the quantity supplied exceeds the demand, a supply surplus occurs. Normally this happens when the market clearing price is above equilibrium.

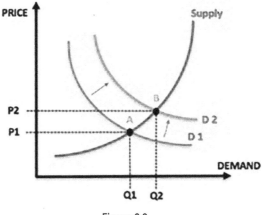

Figure 6.3

Equilibrium is not permanent. In Figure 6.3, there is a shift in demand from D1 to D2. When this happens, there is a change in market equilibrium. Oftentimes this happens when there are nonprice-related changes such as a change in technology or taste of the market.

In the same way, changes in the supply cause a shift in the market clearing price. Figure 6.4 illustrates this as S1 shifts to S2, and market equilibrium changes once again. This is normally accompanied by a drop in the market clearing price.

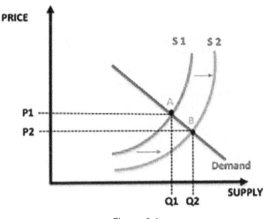

Figure 6.4

Supply can shift to the right if the company's costs fall. For example, if energy prices fall, that will shift the supply curve outward indicating that at the same price, suppliers are willing to supply more goods to the market, in this case because it is cheaper to produce those goods.

In some cases, changes lead to a decrease in demand for a good or service. When this happens, demand contracts, and the demand curve shifts to the left.

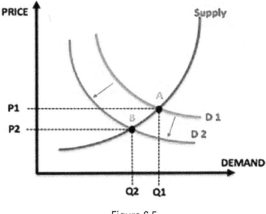

Figure 6.5

Factors that lead to a decrease in demand include:

- changes in tastes and preferences
- fall in the price of substitute goods
- a fall in household income
- introduction of new substitutes
- the price of complementary goods goes up
- consumer expectations discourage buying

The same is true for supply. A decrease in supply can occur for goods and services. As supply contracts, there is often a rise in prices at all levels.

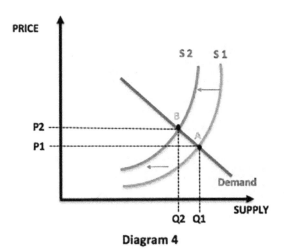

Diagram 4

Figure 6.6

Causes of a decrease in supply include:

- Government regulation: For example, a new regulation that forces firms to spend more money on labels and product descriptions, which will increase production costs.
- Higher taxes: An increase in tax on a product, for example a $2 government tax on all phones, is a cost to business, which would increase price.
- Decline in the availability of the factors of production: For example, a flood wipes out cotton crops. This decreases the supply of cotton shirts.
- A loss of technology needed to produce a good or service: Imagine if we lost the great technological creation of the internet. It would slow many businesses and shut down entire industries that depend on internet communications and sales.

Questions

1. Which of the following changes in the supply of and demand for a good definitely result in a decrease in both the equilibrium price and the quantity of the good?

	Supply	*Demand*
(A)	Increase	Increase
(B)	Increase	No change
(C)	No change	Decrease
(D)	Decrease	Increase
(E)	Decrease	Decrease

Module 7:
The Circular Flow Model

Ever wonder how economies work? In a three-sector economy, households, firms, and the government interact and influence the income flow. In economics, the circular flow model is an easy way to see how sectors of the economy interact within a closed economy.

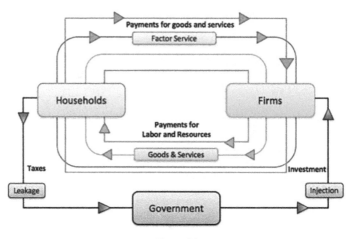

Figure 7.1

Figure 7.1 illustrates the income flow in a three-sector economy.

- Households pay firms for goods and services they purchase.
- Firms supply households with goods and services and pay households for labor and other factors of production.
- The income flow between firms and households illustrates the primary income flow within a closed economy.
- The third sector in Figure 7.1 is the government. Money paid to the government from households is called **leakage** and mainly takes the form of taxes. When

money is not spent on consumption, it is called leakage. Another form of leakage is savings.

- Likewise, injections are types of expenditure on goods and services that do not come from household consumption. In Figure 7.1 the main injection is from the government. Government investment pumps money back into the economy.

Questions

1. In an economy that consist of households and businesses, which of the following is consistent with the circular flow of income and production?

   (A) Households are producers of goods and services and consumers of resources.
   (B) Households are users of resources, and businesses are sources of saving.
   (C) Households are suppliers of resources and consumers of goods and services.
   (D) Businesses are users of taxes, and households are sources of taxes.
   (E) Businesses are suppliers of resources and consumers of goods and services.

Module 8:
Gross Domestic Product

Gross domestic product (GDP) is the broadest measure of economic output and puts a dollar value on all economic transactions in a country. GDP is calculated as:

Consumption + Investment + Government Spending + Net Exports

Consumption

When you purchase a cup of coffee at your favorite coffee shop, or a bicycle, or pay for a haircut or legal services, those transactions are counted as consumption in the calculation of GDP. Any individual and household spending on goods and services is classified as consumption. Consumption increases GDP.

Investment

Let's say a farmer purchases a large package of seeds in the spring and pays a delivery company to ship her goods to market. These business transactions are classified as investment spending in the calculation of GDP. Investment increases GDP.

Government spending may include large-scale federal government expenditure on roads and bridges, or state or provincial spending on schools and hospitals, or city and municipal purchases of emergency flooding supplies, or teacher and firefighter salaries. Government spending increases GDP. Government transfers such as unemployment, maternity, old-age, and low-income benefits do not count toward GDP despite being a form of government spending, because transfer payments such as these are not new forms of spending but simply a redistribution of existing funds.

For example, the United States has the largest army in the world, requiring massive expenditure to keep it running. The purchases of army boots, weapons, aircraft, technology, and services such as banking, engineering, catering and translation are all examples of transactions that are classified as government spending.

Net exports: (Exports - imports)

Exports are sales of goods and services to foreign countries. For example, when a farmer based in Florida sells oranges grown in US to Canadian consumers, this is classified as an export for the United States and increases GDP since it is money coming into the economy from outside the economy.

Imports are purchases of goods and services from foreign countries and deduct from GDP since it means that money is leaving the country. When a British teenager purchases a Nintendo product, that counts as an import for the United Kingdom and an export for Japan, where Nintendo products are made.

What are the limitations of GDP?

As I said earlier, GDP is often used as a measure of the total goods and services produced by an economy. This means it measures all the durable goods, nondurable goods, services, structures, and changes in inventories in an economy, but the GDP is an imperfect measure.

- GDP measures only output produced and sold in the legal market.

- GDP does not account for the black market - illegal market transactions that take place. Trade of drugs, exotic animals, and fake luxury items are just a few examples of black markets.
- GDP is not a good measure of the quality of life within the economy.
- It does not account for productive activities outside the market such as raising children.
- GDP is limited only to productive activity involved in trade, whereas other measures like the quality of people's health, education, and well-being are not considered.
- GDP fails to measure how output affects the quality of people's lives as well as how it affects the environment.
- GDP is a purely quantitative measure, so qualitative aspects of the economy are not considered during the calculation of GDP.

There are three ways of counting GDP: the expenditure method, income method, and production method.

1. The expenditure approach calculates GDP by adding all final goods and services purchased in the economy. You will see this equation a lot in future units.

    GDP = Consumption + Investment + Government Spending + Exports- Imports

2. The income approach looks at the final income made in a country. It adjusts for depreciation, taxes, and subsidies, as only income made from producing goods and services is counted.

    GDP = Wages + Interest on capital+ Rent profits from land ownership + Firm Profits

3. The production (or value added) approach sums up all the value added in different stages of producing goods. This method aims to avoid double counting the value of a product.

    GDP= Final value of all goods and services – Intermediate Costs

Module 9:
Unemployment

Aside from GDP, another way to measure the performance of an economy is by measuring the unemployment rate. When many people cannot find jobs, this may be a sign of an economy not producing at the highest level of efficiency.

The **unemployment rate** is the % of individuals in the labor force who do not have a job, and have been recently looking for work. The **labor force** of an economy is the total number of people who are both employed and unemployed. It is calculated as

LF= All Unemployed People + All Employed People

People who are currently working for pay are employed. Those who are not employed but looking for a job are unemployed. Finally, those who do not have paid employment but are not actively seeking jobs are called **discouraged workers** and not included in the labor force. There are different forms of unemployment; the main ones are frictional unemployment, structural unemployment, and cyclical unemployment.

Frictional unemployment occurs during the time it takes to find a job—for example, the time between when someone quits their job and finds a new one, or when a university graduate finds their first job after leaving school.

Structural unemployment exists when the economy has changed, and there is a difference in the type of skills needed in the job market and the types of skills people have. For example, if a company moves from a manual process to a robotic one, it now needs people who know how to manage the new technology, but the current employees have outdated skills for the manual process.

Cyclical unemployment describes the unemployment that occurs during phases of the business cycle. During a recession, demand for products from consumers is low, and therefore suppliers lay off workers. It is also the deviation of the actual unemployment rate from the natural one.

There is also **seasonal unemployment**, which results from jobs that are available only during certain seasons of the year—for example, a ski instructor.

The **labor force participation rate** is a measure of the total active labor force in the economy. Thus, this measure includes the total of people who are currently employed or those who are actively looking for work. The labor force participation rate is an excellent way to measure how many working-age adults participate in the economy. It is computed with the formula:

$$LFPR = \frac{\textit{(number of people participating in the labor force)}}{\textit{(total number of people eligible to participate in the labor force)}}$$

The unemployment rate is calculated with the following formula:

$$Unemployment\ Rate = \frac{\textit{(number of unemployed persons)}}{\textit{(total number of people in the labor force)}}$$

How do changes in the labor market affect unemployment?

- The remaining level of unemployment when an economy is healthy is called the **natural rate of unemployment**. This is caused by economic, social, and political factors that exist within a given stable economy. It is made up of only frictional and structural unemployment. The rate could never be zero, because even if an economy is producing efficient levels of output, there is always some level of unemployment.
- In any economy job creation and job destruction lead to changes in the number of people employed. When companies expand and contract their workforce or when social and economic forces shift, the unemployment rate changes.
- Structural changes in society often lead to job losses as well as the creation of new jobs. One such structural change that is easy to identify is the shift to automation in recent times. Machines have replaced traditional human jobs in many industries, displacing many workers who will have to retrain and reskill in order to find work in other industries.

Limitations of the Unemployment Rate

The unemployment rate is not a perfect measure. It is often said to understate the level of unemployment:

- It does not account for discouraged workers or marginally attached workers.
- There is no separation between full-time and part-time workers.
- The wage levels are not taken into consideration. Even though someone is employed, they may be making less money than needed to have a proper standard of living.
- It also does not capture the long-run unemployment rate or how long someone has been unemployed.

Questions

1. Which of the following individuals is considered officially unemployed?

   (A) Chris, who has not worked for more than three years and has given up looking for work
   (B) Kim, who is going to school full-time and is waiting until graduation before looking for a job
   (C) Pat, who recently left a job to look for a different job in another town
   (D) Leslie, who retired after turning sixty-five only five months ago
   (E) Lee, who is working twenty hours per week and is seeking full-time employment

2. The unemployment rate is calculated as

   (A) the number of people not working divided by the population.
   (B) the number of people not working divided by the number of people working both full-time and part-time.
   (C) the number of people working part-time but actively seeking full-time employment divided by the number of people in the labor force.
   (D) the number of people not working but actively seeking employment divided by the number of people in the labor force.
   (E) the number of people in the labor force divided by the population.

3. When an economy is in equilibrium at potential GDP, the actual unemployment rate is

   (A) equal to the cyclical rate.
   (B) greater than the natural rate.
   (C) less than the natural rate.

(D) equal to the natural rate.

(E) equal to zero.

4. Countries face trade-offs between producing consumer goods and producing capital goods.

The following table shows labor-market data for country X.

Employed	180,000
Frictionally unemployed	10,000
Structurally unemployed	5,000
Cyclically unemployed	5,000
Not in the labor force	100,000

(i)   Calculate the unemployment rate in country X. Show your work.

(ii) Calculate the labor force participation rate in country X. Show your work.

5. Assume the expected inflation rate in a country is 3 percent, the current unemployment rate is 6 percent, and the natural rate of unemployment is 4 percent. Based on the relationship between the actual and the expected inflation rates, what will happen to the natural rate of unemployment in the long run?

Module 10:

Prices and Inflation

Inflation is the term used to describe an increase in prices.

To compute the inflation rate: $\pi, \pi = 100 \; x \; \dfrac{CPI_1 - CPI_0}{CPI_0}$.

Inflation is natural and ongoing in every economy. Individuals and businesses are constantly competing for goods and services, and suppliers are constantly seeking opportunities to increase profits through raising prices. Real variables are variables that are adjusted for inflation or price changes.

In nominal variables inflation and prices have not been taken into consideration. *Keep this in mind when we talk about nominal or real interest rates.*

In contrast, **deflation** happens when the rate of inflation is below 0 percent. Deflation causes the prices of goods and services to fall. Deflation slows down economic growth because the demand for goods and services is lower than normal. When there is a temporary slowing of the pace of price inflation, it is called **disinflation**. Unlike deflation, disinflation describes a drop in the rate of inflation. Prices do not normally fall during a period of disinflation.

The **consumer price index (CPI)** is a common way governments measure inflation. It shows the change in income someone would need to keep their standard of living while experiencing different price levels. It is measured with the formula:

$$CPI = \dfrac{Cost \; of \; Market \; Basket \; in \; Given \; Year}{Cost \; of \; Market \; Basket \; in \; Base \; Year} \; x \; 100$$

It uses a base year to compare other years.

In the United States, the government calculates the CPI based on a **fixed basket of goods**, which is a set of consumer products and services valued every year.

27

How to Compute CPI and Inflation

Sample economy of four goods:

Year	Qty bread	Price bread	Qty jeans	Price jeans	Qty petrol	Price petrol	Qty newspaper	Price newspaper
2018	10	$0.60	10	$15	15	$2.50	10	$2.50
2019	15	$0.75	10	$16	15	$3	12	$2.75
2020	20	$0.90	10	$18	25	$3.5	16	$3.20

Basket of goods using 2018 prices = 10($0.60)+5($15)+10($2.50)+10($2.50)

Basket of goods using 2018 prices = $218

Basket of goods using 2019 prices = 15($0.75)+10($16)+15($3)+12($2.75)

Basket of goods using 2019 prices = $249.25

The CPI for 2019 is calculated as $CPI = \dfrac{\$249.25}{\$218} \times 100 = 114.22$

Basket of goods using 2019 prices = 15($0.75)+10($16)+15($3)+12($2.75)

Basket of goods using 2019 prices = $249.25

Basket of goods using 2020 prices = 20($0.90)+10($18)+25($3.5)+16($3.20)

Basket of goods using 2020 prices = $336.7

The CPI for 2020 is calculated as $CPI = \dfrac{\$336.7}{\$249.25} \times 100 = 134.80$

Inflation rate is $\pi = 100 \times \dfrac{134.80-114.22}{114.22} = 18\%$

Shortcomings of CPI

The **substitution bias** is a shortcoming of the CPI. The CPI often overstates inflation because it does not account for the substitution effect. Some prices rise faster than others, and consumers substitute these goods for cheaper ones. However, the CPI focuses only on a fixed basket of goods, which causes it to miss this substitution method.

The CPI does not account for improvements in products and services, which may validate the price increases. For example, a fridge could have cost $400 twenty years ago, but now it costs $1000. However, it now includes things like a touchscreen and energy saving capabilities, which cost more.

Costs of Inflation

Unexpected inflation rates can have a negative impact on individuals and the economy.

1. A country's products are less competitive when it has a significantly *higher inflation rate than its trading partners*. This often leads to less competitive exports, because the prices are relatively higher.

2. *Shoe leather costs:* When prices rise, it causes more transactions to take place. For example, if prices are higher, you may need to go to the ATM more often than before and face ATM fees as a result.

3. *Menu costs:* It can get expensive for businesses to constantly update their prices in the face of hyperinflation (astronomically high prices).

4. *Unit of account costs:* When prices are rising at high rates, it makes money a less reliable measure of value.

Inflation can also lead to certain parties benefiting. If you borrowed money and owe someone, you will gain from inflation because you will be paying back the same amount of money that is technically now worth more. If you are on the other side, and you are a lender, you will lose on inflation. The money you will receive from the borrower now is worth less and has less purchasing power than when you lent it out.

Questions

1. (i) If in one year the price index is 50, and in the next year the price index is 55, what is the rate of inflation from one year to the next?

   (ii) Assume that next year's wage rate will be 3 percent higher than this year's because of inflationary expectations. The actual inflation rate is 4 percent. At the beginning of next year, will the real wage be higher, lower, or the same as today?

2. Hyperinflation is typically caused by

    (A) high tax rates that discourage work effort.
    (B) continuous expansion of the money supply to finance government budget deficits.
    (C) trade surpluses that are caused by strong protectionist policies.
    (D) bad harvests that lead to widespread shortages.
    (E) a large decline in corporate profits that leads to a decrease in production.

3. The CPI is designed to measure changes in the

    (A) spending patterns of urban consumers only.
    (B) spending patterns of all consumers.
    (C) wholesale price of manufactured goods.
    (D) prices of all goods and services produced in an economy.
    (E) cost of a select market basket of goods and services.

4. The CPI measures the

    (A) value of current GDP in base-year dollars.
    (B) prices of all consumer goods and services produced in the economy.
    (C) prices of selected raw materials purchased by firms.
    (D) prices of a specific group of goods and services purchased by consumers.
    (E) prices of imports but not exports.

Module 11:
Real vs. Nominal GDP

Nominal GDP is concerned with measuring the total dollar value of all the output of an economy at current market prices. Nominal GDP computes GDP based on current prices in the year in which the goods and services were produced.

The nominal GDP as a measure of economic growth is flawed, because it has the tendency to overstate the growth of output since it does not take the changes in prices into consideration.

Real GDP focuses on measuring the value of all final goods and services produced in an economy during a given year. Real GDP compares production between two years using a base price for all goods and services produced in the economy.

To compute the real GDP, use the formula $R = \dfrac{N}{D}$, where N is nominal GDP and D is the deflator. For example, calculate the real GDP for 2019 if the nominal GDP is $102.10 billion and the deflator was 1.134.

The **GDP Deflator** is a tool used to measure the level of price changes over a period of time, allowing current prices to be comparable to historical prices.

Use the formula $R = \dfrac{N}{D}$.

$$R = \frac{\$102.10}{1.134}$$

R=$90.0353 billion

The example illustrates the flaw of using only the nominal GDP to measure economic growth for the economy. The nominal GDP normally inflates GDP growth because it uses current prices and does not consider that prices tend to increase year after year.

Questions

1.

	2009 Quantity	2009 Price (base year)	2010 Quantity	2010 Price
Food	6	$2.5	8	$2.5
Clothes	5	$6	10	$10
Entertainment	2	$4	5	$5

The outputs and prices of goods and services in country X are shown in the table. Assuming that 2009 is the base year, calculate each of the following.

(i) The nominal gross domestic product (GDP) in 2010
(ii) The real GDP in 2010

2. Which of the following best illustrates an improvement in a country's standard of living?

(A) An increase in real per capita GDP
(B) An increase in nominal per capita GDP
(C) Price stability
(D) A balanced budget
(E) An increase in the consumer price index

Period	Real GDP	Nominal GDP
Year 1	$100 billion	$70 billion
Year 2	$120 billion	$120 billion
Year 3	$130 billion	$150 billion

3. Which of the following can be concluded from the data above?

(A) The base year for the price index was year 1.
(B) The base year for the price index was year 3.
(C) The economy was producing higher-quality goods and services in years 2 and 3 than in year 1.
(D) The economy was experiencing inflation during years 2 and 3.
(E) The economy was experiencing deflation during years 1, 2, and 3.

Module 12:

Business Cycle

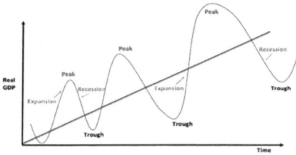

Figure 12.1

Note: the wavelike grey line is actual RGDP, while the upward sloping red line is the long run trend of growth.

The business cycle follows a wavelike pattern that shows the rise and fall in the production of goods and services in the economy and the economy's short-term movement in and out of recession. Figure 12.1 shows the business cycle of an economy.

Between 1994 and 2000, the commercialization of the internet made online companies extremely popular in the United States. The dot.com companies became extremely popular among consumers and investors, leading to a boom in trade. In fact, the US economy experienced significant economic growth in the 1990s. This period illustrates the rise in business activity within the economy called **expansion**. In Figure 12.1 expansions are periods in the economy characterized by economic upturn. The highest point of growth during a period of expansion is called the **peak**. The popularity of the dot.com industry reached its peak by 2000.

Conversely, **recessions** occur when economic activity is in decline. This is a period characterized by falling output and employment. In Figure 12.1 recessions occur following peaks. Each phase of the business cycle is made of an expansion phase and a recession phase. The highest point of phase is called the peak; the lowest point is the trough.

The business cycle of an economy follows a pattern of expansions and contractions of economic output and employment. It is influenced by changes in aggregate supply and aggregate demand. Potential output is also called full-employment output, and it is the level of GDP or output the economy could produce if it was operating at full capacity and efficiency.

The business cycle experiences **output gaps**, the difference between the actual output and the potential output of an economy. It can be a positive gap, when the economy is operating above the full level of employment, or a negative gap, when the economy is operating above the full level of employment).

Questions

1.   Which of the following describes a typical business cycle in the correct sequence?

    (A) Peak, trough, recession, and expansion
    (B) Peak, trough, expansion, and recession
    (C) Peak, recession, trough, and expansion
    (D) Peak, recession, expansion, and trough
    (E) Peak, expansion, trough, and recession

Module 13:
The Multiplier

When President Barack Obama passed a large trillion dollar plus spending bill to counteract the 2008/2009 recession, he promised this initial spending would provide ripple benefits throughout the economy for years to come. He was referring to the power of the multiplier effect. While $1 of new spending in an economy may seem to increase GDP initially by only $1, that $1 actually also increases **disposable income**, which is the amount of money individuals have to spend after taxes. That rise in disposable income will lead to a second round of impact on GDP when a part of it is spent on a good or service. So the actual impact on GDP of that new $1 in spending is more than $1.

We assume in macroeconomics that individuals can do two things with their money: spend or save it. The amount of each dollar that individuals generally spend is referred to as the marginal propensity to consume (MPC). It is calculated by the change in consumption over the change in income.

$$MPC= \Delta C/ \Delta Y$$

The remainder of each dollar earned that is not spent is saved. This is called the marginal propensity to save (MPS).

$$MPC+MPS=1$$

The **expenditure multiplier** quantifies the size of the change in aggregate demand that results from a change in any of the four components of aggregate demand. The simple **spending multiplier** is calculated as (1/(1-MPC). The **tax multiplier** (-MPC/(1-MPC) quantifies the size of the change in aggregate demand that results from a change in taxes.

The tax multiplier causes a smaller change in GDP relative to the expenditure multiplier because people tend to save some of the tax cuts and pay tax increases by both less spending and saving less. Therefore the tax multiplier is smaller than the expenditure multiplier.

Example:

MPC is 0.8, which means 80 percent of each additional dollar is spent, not saved. MPS is therefore 0.2, which means 20 percent of each additional dollar is saved, not spent.

Let's assume the federal government passes a $500 billion spending bill to boost economic growth, such as the one passed by the Obama Administration in 2009. The first round of this $500 billion increases the GDP by $500 billion. This $500 billion becomes disposable income for many economic actors, such as government contractors who spend money on corporations and small and medium-sized businesses that purchase raw materials from farmers and other small businesses, etc.

These actors won't spend all of this newly acquired income, only 80 percent of it, or $400 million in the second round of impact. The third round would be 80 percent of the previous $400 million from the second round, or $320 million. This goes on and on. The easiest way to calculate the total expenditure multiplier is to use the formula (1/1-MPC). In this case, 1/[1-0.8] or 1/0.2, which is equal to 5. An expenditure multiplier of five means that an increase in new spending by $1 will increase GDP by $5.

Try this out on your own below, using other numbers.

Questions

1. Which of the following best explains the increase in national income that results from equal increases in government spending and taxes?

   (A) Consumers do not reduce their spending by the full amount of a tax increase.
   (B) The government purchases some goods that consumers would have purchased on their own.
   (C) Consumers believe all tax cuts are transitory.
   (D) The increase in government spending causes a decrease in investment.
   (E) Consumers are aware of tax increases but not of increases in government spending.

2. Suppose in an economy with lump-sum taxes and no international trade, autonomous investment spending increases by $2 million. If the marginal propensity to consume is 0.75, equilibrium GDP will change by a maximum of

   (A) $0.5 million.
   (B) $1.5 million.
   (C) $2.0 million.
   (D) $8.0 million.
   (E) $15.0 million.

3. If the marginal propensity to consume is 0.9, the government increases purchases by $100, and net exports decline by $60, the equilibrium level of real GDP will

   (A) decrease by up to $400.
   (B) increase by up to $400.
   (C) increase by up to $600.
   (D) decrease by up to $1600.
   (E) increase by up to $1600.

4. Assume the United States economy is currently operating below the full-employment level of real GDP with a balanced budget.

   If the marginal propensity to consume is 0.75, calculate the maximum possible change in real GPD that could result from the $100 billion increase in government spending.

5. Canada is an open economy that is currently in a recessionary output gap. Suppose the Canadian government is unwilling to wait for the long-run adjustment process.

The marginal propensity to consume is 0.8. The equilibrium real output is $500 billion, and the full-employment output is $540 billion.

(i)   Calculate the minimum change and indicate the direction of change in government spending required to shift the aggregate demand curve by the amount of the output gap.

(ii) Calculate the minimum change and indicate the direction of change in taxes required to shift the aggregate demand curve by the amount of the output gap.

Aggregate Demand & Aggregate Supply Model

Aggregate Demand

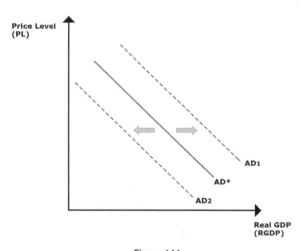

Figure 14.1

An increase in aggregate demand (AD) is illustrated as a shift outward, or to the right. A decrease in AD is illustrated as a shift inward, or to the left. Reminder: AD, or real GDP, comprises consumption, investment, government spending, and net exports.

The AD curve illustrates the negative relationship between AD and real GDP. A movement from A to B along the AD curve reflects lower price levels and higher real GDP. But why is the AD curve negatively sloped?

- ○ The wealth effect (higher prices reduce purchasing power): When overall price levels rise, the purchasing power of individuals falls. People can't afford as many goods and services assuming all else, like income, remains the same.

- ○ The exchange rate effect: Higher price levels make local goods and services more expensive to foreign buyers, which can reduce exports. Lower exports reduce AD, all else being equal.
- ○ The interest rate effect: Figure 14.2

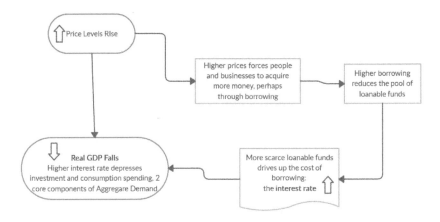

Figure 14.2

Shifters of Aggregate Demand

Shifter	Example	Impact on AD curve
More wealth [*]	If the stock market experiences a boom, households have more wealth, and AD increases because with more wealth, households spend more, boosting the consumption part of GDP.	AD shifts to the right, or outward.
Less wealth	In 2008 home prices in the United States fell dramatically, reducing the wealth of many households. Less wealth discourages spending.	AD shifts to the left, or inward.

The size of the existing stock of physical capital is small.	If a retail clothing store has very little inventory left, that store will have to request more goods to sell, which will spur the factories to produce more products to provide to the retailer, which boosts AD since businesses must purchase raw materials and pay laborers to create these goods.	AD shifts to the right, or outward.
The size of the existing stock of physical capital is large.	If that retail clothing store fills its inventories but does not experience a major increase in sales to deplete the stock of clothing, the retailer will not make any requests for more goods from factories in the near future, which means suppliers of these goods will have to produce less in the short run until inventory is depleted. Producing less means less purchases of raw materials and payments to laborers.	AD shifts to the left, or inward.
Fiscal policy: Government spending increases.	If the government decides to pass a law increasing spending on infrastructure, it will lead to an increase in government purchases on building new infrastructure, which will involve hiring contractors and purchasing equipment, which will increase overall spending in the economy.	AD shifts to the right, or outward.
Fiscal policy: Taxation increases.	If the government increases income taxes, individual workers will have less money to spend on goods and services and will spend less, all else being equal.	AD shifts to the left, or inward.

Expansionary monetary policy: Reduce reserve requirements. Reduce discount rate. Buy government bonds.	During a recession, the Federal Reserve usually engages in expansionary activities, boosting the money supply, which reduces interest rates. Lower interest rates encourage borrowing and therefore increase consumption and investment spending.	AD shifts to the right, or outward.
Contractionary monetary policy: Sell government bonds. Increase discount rate. Increase reserve requirements.	When inflation starts to rise to high levels, the Federal Reserve may want to reduce the supply of money in the economy by selling government bonds and therefore increasing the interest rate, which depresses spending and investment.	AD shifts to the left, or inward.
Better expectations for the future	If people feel confident that their future income will rise, they will be more comfortable making purchases now, boosting overall expenditures.	AD shifts to the right, or outward.
Lesser expectations for the future	If recession fears are in the news every day, and businesses everywhere are starting to lay off workers, individuals and businesses may feel more pessimistic about the future; believing their incomes may not necessarily rise and may even fall. This will depress current consumption and investment, as economic actors hold off on transactions in fear of economic decline.	AD shifts to the left or inward

Wealth is different from income. Income refers to the money made in a given period, say the salary a police officer makes in a given year. That police officer's total wealth, however, includes accumulated income and assets over the course of his life. Although his income may have been $31,000 in 2019, his wealth includes the value of his car, home, paintings, and jewelry.

Questions on Aggregate Demand

1. A US firm sells $10 million worth of goods to a firm in Argentina, where the currency is the peso.

    How will the transaction affect Argentina's AD? Explain.

2. An increase in which of the following would cause the AD curve to shift to the left?

    (A) Consumer optimism
    (B) Population
    (C) Cost of resources
    (D) Income taxes
    (E) Net exports

3. One explanation for the downward slope of the AD curve is that when the price level rises, which of the following decreases?

    (A) Real value of assets
    (B) Prices of foreign goods
    (C) Prices of substitute goods
    (D) Expectations of future prices
    (E) Government deficit

4. The AD curve is downward sloping because an rise in the general price level will cause the demand for money, interest rates, and investment to change in which of the following ways?

	Demand for Money	Interest Rates	Investment
(A)	Increase	Increase	Increase
(B)	Increase	Increase	Decrease
(C)	Increase	Decrease	Increase
(D)	Decrease	Increase	Decrease
(E)	Decrease	Decrease	Increase

5. Assume the US economy is in recession.

Now assume the Euro zone, a major trading partner of the United States, enters into a recession.

    (i)   What will be the effect on US exports to the Euro zone? Explain.

    (ii) On your graph in part (a), show the effect of the change identified in part (b)(i) on real output in the United States.

    (iii) What will be the effect of the change identified in part (b)(ii) on unemployment in the United States?

Aggregate Supply

Fixed costs are costs companies face that do not change, no matter the level of output. Example: A bakery has to pay rent every month, regardless of how much cookies and cake it sells. Rent for a bakery is therefore a fixed cost.

Variable cost change depending on the level of a business's output. That same bakery has to purchase flour every time it bakes a cake; therefore, the cost of this *raw material* increases depending on how many cake orders the store gets. If the store gets zero orders, the cost of flour is $0, assuming the store buys flour only when an order comes in for cake. If the store gets 100 orders for cake, and has to pay $1 per cake for flour, the cost is $100.

When economists say long run, they mean long term, or a lot of time—enough time for there to be nothing permanent. Businesses looking at their long-term outlook are able to make substantial changes to their operations, including changing locations and factory sizes. *There are no fixed costs in the long run; all costs are variable. They can change with time.* In the short run, however, time is limited, which means businesses are not as flexible to make changes to their business structures or sizes. Therefore, in the short run, there are both fixed and variable costs.

Short-Run Aggregate Supply

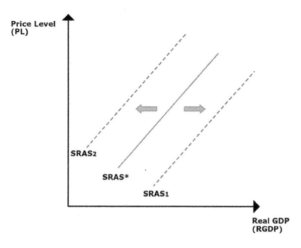

Figure 14.3

An increase in the short-run aggregate supply (SRAS) is illustrated as a shift outward, or to the right. A decrease in the SRAS is illustrated as a shift inward, or to the left. The SRAS curve illustrates the positive relationship between price levels and real GDP. A movement from A to B along the SRAS curve reflects inflation—higher price levels but also a rise in real GDP.

When real GDP is higher, unemployment is lower. A movement along the SRAS curve suggests that at higher prices (inflation), unemployment is lower and output is higher, which requires more labor. When prices are lower, unemployment is higher, since output is lower.

Why is it upward sloping? The SRAS curve slopes up due to sticky wages (input) and sticky prices (output). This is the theory that workers' earnings and prices do not adjust quickly to market conditions in the short run. For example, due to contracts, they cannot completely respond to changes such as inflation or deflation fast.

Shifters of SRAS

Shifter	Example	Impact on SRAS curve
Increase in production costs	When energy prices rise (e.g., oil and gas—or raw materials for most economic activity, it drives up costs for businesses and reduces their ability to produce as much. Expectations that production costs will rise can also have the effect of reducing business output.	SRAS decreases: Shifts to the left, or inward
Decrease in production costs	When the price of a common commodity like corn falls, the costs for producers who use corn fall, increasing the producers' ability to produce.	SRAS increase: Shifts to the right, or outward
Increase in nominal wages	Labor unions, also known as trade unions, regularly petition companies to increase wages on behalf of their member employees. During strong economic conditions, they may be very successful at doing so, helping to boost employees' wages. This makes it more expensive for businesses to produce, however, and reduces business output.	SRAS decrease: Shifts to the left, or inward
Decrease in nominal wages	An oversupply of labor in certain labor markets can suppress wages based on the principle of supply and demand. Lower wages make it more profitable for businesses, since their costs are lower. Lower wages also encourage businesses to produce more to capture this increased profit.	SRAS increases: Shift outward, or to the right

Productivity improvements	New technology that makes it easier to produce for many businesses would increase overall output. Take the internet, for example: the internet made it much easier for businesses to sell to customers and caused a significant boost to GDP, particularly in the 1990s and early 2000s.	SRAS increases: Shifts to the right, or outward
Fall in productivity	If there was an electrical outage that affected 40 percent of the population for over a year, it would have a devastating impact on business output.	SRAS decreases: Shifts to the left, or inward

Long-Run Aggregate Supply

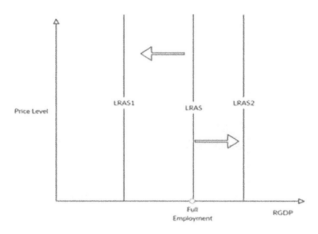

Figure 14.4

The long-run aggregate supply (LRAS) curve is vertical, suggesting that in the long term, output is fixed at a certain level, when all economic resources are used. It can be compared to the production possibilities curve (PPC) because they both reflect the highest possible level of output with the available resources. An increase or decrease in the LRAS is caused by the same factors that may increase or decrease the PPC: population, productivity, land, etc.

The LRAS intersects the x-axis at the level of real GDP that provides full employment; that is, everyone who wants a job has one. This is because in the long run, wages and prices fully adjust.

Short-Run Equilibrium

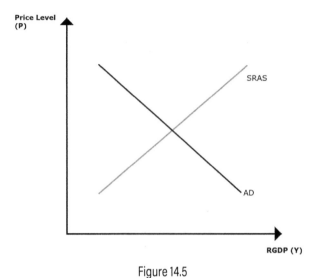

Figure 14.5

Long-Run Equilibrium

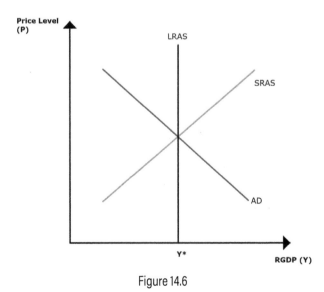

Figure 14.6

The long-run equilibrium occurs where the LRAS curve intersects the short-run equilibrium, where AD and SRAS meet.

Inflationary Gap

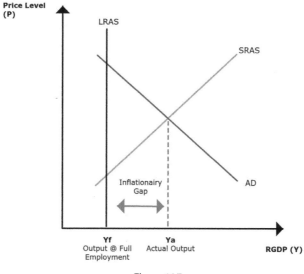

Figure 14.7

When the short-run aggregate supply and aggregate demand curves intersect at a point on the x-axis above the level of output at full employment, the economy is experiencing an inflationary gap. Real output is above the long-term sustainable level, and unemployment is low. As a matter of fact, there are usually shortages of labor during an inflationary gap.

Recessionary Gap

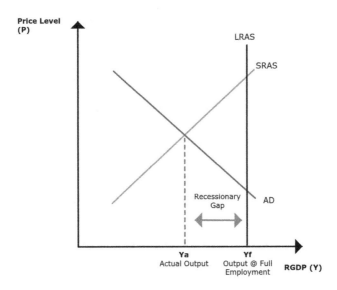

Figure 14.8

When the short-run aggregate supply and aggregate demand curves intersect at a point on the x-axis below the level of output at full employment, the economy is experiencing a recessionary gap. Real output is below the long-term sustainable level, and unemployment is high. Many people who are looking for work are unable to find it.

Questions

6. With an upward-sloping SRAS curve, an increase in government expenditure will most likely

    (A) reduce the price level.
    (B) reduce the level of nominal GDP.
    (C) increase real GDP.
    (D) shift the short-run aggregate supply curve to the right.
    (E) shift both the aggregate demand curve and the LRAS curve to the left.

7. A simultaneous increase in inflation and unemployment could be explained by an increase in which of the following?

    (A) Consumer spending
    (B) The money supply

(C) Labor productivity

(D) Investment spending

(E) Inflationary expectations

8.   With an upward-sloping aggregate supply curve, an increase in the money supply will affect the price level and real GDP in the short run in which of the following ways?

	Price Level	Real GDP
(A)	Decrease	Decrease
(B)	Decrease	Increase
(C)	Increase	Decrease
(D)	Increase	Increase
(E)	No change	No change

9.   An increase in which of the following is most likely to cause the SRAS curve to shift to the left?

(A) Consumers' incomes

(B) The money supply

(C) Government spending

(D) The optimism of business firms

(E) The per unit cost of production

Changes to the AD-AS Model in the Short Run

The section on AD and AS lists all of the relevant shifters of the AD and SRAS curves. Positive shifters increase AD and shift out the curve to the right, whereas negative shifters or shocks shift the curve to the left.

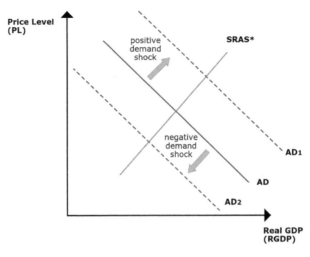

Figure 14.9

A positive demand shock causes the short-run equilibrium to rise; both price levels and real GDP increase. This rise in prices caused by a positive demand shock is referred to as **demand-pull inflation.**

A negative demand shock causes the short-run equilibrium to fall. AD meets SRAS at a lower real GDP level; price levels also fall as a result.

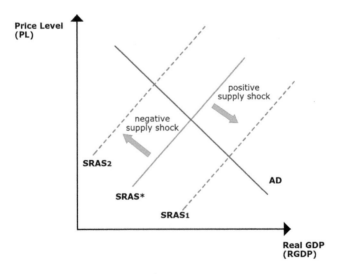

Figure 14.10

A negative supply shock shifts the SRAS curve to the left, causing the curve to intersect AD at a higher price level and lower real GDP. The increase in prices caused by this negative supply shock is referred to as **cost-push inflation.**

A positive supply shock shifts the SRAS curve to the right, causing the curve to intersect the AD curve at a lower price level and higher real GDP.

Long-Run Self-Adjustment in the AS-AD Model

Self-Adjustment: Inflationary Gap

- An inflationary gap causes a rise in wages.
- Higher wages increase business costs, which reduces aggregate supply.
- A lower aggregate supply is illustrated as a shift in the SRAS curve.
- This reduction in the AS occurs until the real GDP level is equal to the long-run equilibrium level of real output.

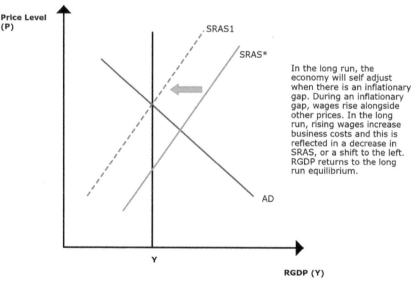

Figure 14.11

Self-Adjustment: Recessionary Gap

- A recessionary gap causes a fall in prices overall.
- Lower prices reduce business costs, which increases aggregate supply. Remember, higher prices incentivize business to produce more.

- A higher AS is illustrated as a shift out of the SRAS curve.
- This outward shift occurs until the real GDP level is equal to the long-run equilibrium level of real output.

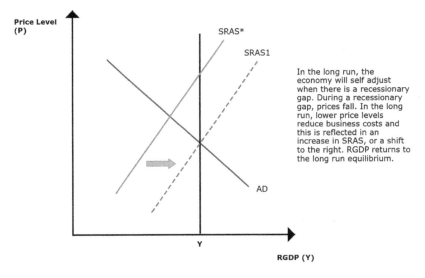

Figure 14.12

Questions

10. Assume that an economy is currently in long-run equilibrium, and the SRAS curve is upward sloping. An adverse supply shock such as a drought will most likely cause which of the following to the economy in the short run?

    (A) A decrease in the price level and a decrease in the nominal wage
    (B) A decrease in the price level and an increase in the nominal wage
    (C) An increase in the price level and an increase in the nominal wage
    (D) An increase in the price level and an increase in the real wage
    (E) An increase in the price level and a decrease in the real wage

11. Which of the following would cause both the AS and AS curves to shift to the right?

    (A) A decrease in corporate income taxes
    (B) A decrease in government spending
    (C) A decrease in natural resource prices
    (D) A decrease in the stock market prices
    (E) An increase in the international value of the domestic currency

12. Assume the economy is in long-run equilibrium. A shift in the AD curve will change

    (A) only the price level in the long run.

    (B) only the output level in the long run.

    (C) both the price level and the output level in the long run.

    (D) neither the price level nor the output level in the short run.

    (E) only the price level in the short run and only the output level in the long run.

Fiscal Policy

$GDP = C + I + \mathbf{G} + NX$

Fiscal policies are the what government uses to fund itself and to achieve its objectives through government spending. Governments use these policies to manage economic output, employment, and inflation rates. The government uses two primary tools in fiscal policy.

Government taxation (taxes) provides the government with the money it needs to operate. In many developed countries, a typical individual may pay a wide variety of taxes: income taxes, sales taxes on goods and services, property taxes, and even upon death an estate tax.

Government expenditure (spending) on policy objectives comes from money the government earns in taxation and, in some cases, money it borrows. Governments provide a variety of public goods and services, often free of charge: hospitals, roads, schools, shelters, universities, libraries, public housing, and many others.

Government transfers are a redistributive element. The government redistributes wealth and income by using the taxes of wealthier individuals to handle social issues such as poverty, child care, elderly care, unemployment, and income inequalities. Government uses tools such as maternity and child-care benefits, older adult benefits such as a monthly check after age sixty-five, monthly payments to individuals who have lost their jobs, payments to individuals who make comparatively low salaries, and so on. These transfer payments do not count toward GDP, as they are simply redistributions of income, not new income.

Changes in Fiscal Policy Affect Aggregate Demand

When the government increases government spending or reduces taxation, such as during a recession, it causes an increase in AD, or a shift to the right of the AD curve.

Ronald Reagan, the fortieth president of the United States, served during the '80s and ran on an economic promise to reduce the size of government by, among other things, reducing government spending. Reductions in government spending decrease AD, causing a shift inward in the AD curve, or a shift to the left.

The Government Spending Multiplier Is Greater than the Tax Multiplier

Fiscal policy has a multiplier effect, but the effect depends on the tool of fiscal policy used. When the government reduces taxation, individuals save some of their new disposable income. When there is an autonomous increase in government spending—that is, a new injection of funds into the economy—the entire amount of the increase affects the economy directly; none of it is saved in the first round of spending.

Expansionary Fiscal Policy

Policies meant to increase AD, real GDP and price levels:

- Increase in government spending on goods and services
- Increase in government transfers (e.g., during the 2009 recession, the US government extended unemployment benefits for millions of Americans for whom it was about to expire)
- Tax cuts

Contractionary Fiscal Policy

Policies meant to reduce price level and/or AD and real GDP:

- Reduction in government spending on goods and services
- Reduction in government transfers
- Increase in taxes

Side Note: Policy Lag

Governments are not known to act quickly. It takes a long time for most governments to react to a major economic issue; it can take years to deal with the politics of introducing legislation and even more time to implement the legislation if successful. In addition, regular delays occur in the legislative process. This phenomenon causes policy lags such that by the time a policy actually takes effect, the economy could be in a completely different part of its business cycle.

The AD–AS model demonstrates the short-run effects of fiscal policy.

Any fiscal policy that impacts consumption, investment, government spending, or net exports moves the AD curve. Expansionary policy shifts AD to the right; contractionary shifts it to the left.

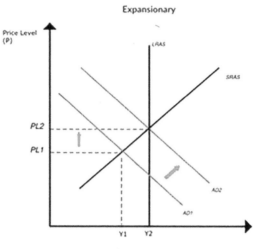

Figure 15.1

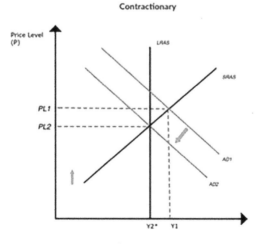

Figure 15.2

Automatic Stabilizers

Intentional government polices to increase or reduce AD are part of a concept known as autonomous changes in government spending. However, automatic changes take place regardless of what the government does.

Tax revenue decreases automatically when GDP falls; less economic activity automatically means governments collect less money from citizens. When the economy is booming, tax revenue automatically increases, since there is more activity to tax. During a recession, unemployment benefits automatically increase due to the rise in unemployment. During an economic boom, unemployment benefits fall automatically when the unemployment rate falls.

Many government agencies that address a variety of social problems that rise during periods of high unemployment automatically spend more when there is a recession. For example, government-sponsored shelters and antipoverty programs may increase spending during a recession without any new policy being enacted.

Government savings
= Tax revenue- government spending - (loan + (loan × interest rate))

Questions

1. The unemployment rate in the country of Southland is greater than the natural rate of unemployment. The president of Southland is receiving advice from two economic advisers—Kohelis and Raymond—about how best to reduce unemployment in Southland. Kohelis advises the president to decrease personal income taxes.

    (i)   How would such a decrease in taxes affect AD?
    (ii) Using a correctly labeled graph of the short-run Phillips curve, show the effect of the decrease in taxes. Label the initial equilibrium as point A and the new equilibrium resulting from the decrease in taxes as point B.

2. Which of the following combinations of changes in government spending and taxes is necessarily expansionary?

    Government | Spending Taxes
    (A) Increase | Increase
    (B) Increase | Decrease
    (C) Decrease | No change
    (D) Decrease | Increase
    (E) Decrease | Decrease

3.   Which of the following policy combinations could reduce a government deficit without changing aggregate demand?

   (A) An increase in taxes and a decrease in the money supply
   (B) An increase in taxes and an increase in the money supply
   (C) A decrease in taxes and a decrease in the money supply
   (D) A decrease in government spending and a decrease in the money supply
   (E) An increase in government spending and a decrease in the money supply

4.   Expansionary fiscal policy will most likely result in

   (A) a decrease in the money supply.
   (B) an increase in the marginal propensity to consume.
   (C) an increase in nominal interest rates.
   (D) a decrease in the level of output.
   (E) a decrease in the price level.

Module 16:

Financial Assets

When you save money, you are participating in the financial system, which links borrowers and lenders. An **asset** is something you own that has value. Your home, car, or a company's machinery are all assets that can be converted into money in the future. A financial asset is an agreement to receive income as the buyer from the seller in the future. There are many types of financial assets, but I will focus on four main ones:

- ○ **Loans:** Money borrowed and expected to be paid back, usually with interest. Loans are assets to banks because even though they lent the money out, it still belongs to them.
- ○ **Stocks:** Claims to ownership of a portion of a company. Stocks pay dividends.
- ○ **Bonds:** IOUs from the issuer of bonds to the purchaser with an agreement to pay interest in a given time frame and repay the principal at a given date.
- ○ **Loan-backed securities:** Assets that promise to pay the holder the payments received from loan holders.

Liquidity refers to an asset's ability to be used right away. Cash is the most liquid, alongside demand deposits (bank accounts from which you can make payments through checks or debit cards). Something like a real estate takes time to become liquid.

A **liability** is an obligation to pay money in the future. The price of previously issued bonds and interest rates on bonds are inversely related. The opportunity cost of holding money is the interest that could have been earned from holding other financial assets such as bonds. The rate of return or return on investment is the gain (or loss) on an investment. It measures the growth of an investment between two periods.

RoR= (new value – old value/old value) x100

Financial risk occurs when the outcome of the value of an asset is unknown or there is uncertainty for the future. Investment spending comes from savings. When you get paid, you can do two things with the money: spend or save it. Anything that is an investment spending (I) comes from savings (S). Therefore, I=S.

Note:

Some students may need to review net present value, and future value as well.

Questions

1. If the annual interest rate is 5 percent, then the present value of $1.00 received one year from now is closest to

    (A) $1.50.
    (B) $1.05.
    (C) $1.00.
    (D) $0.95.
    (E)$0.05.

2. Assume the US economy is in long-run equilibrium with an expected inflation rate of 6 percent and an unemployment rate of 5 percent. The nominal interest rate is 8 percent. Calculate the real interest rate in the long-run equilibrium.

3. Inflation and expected inflation are important determinants of economic activity. Given the increase in the expected rate of inflation from question 2,

    (i) Will the nominal interest rate on new loans increase, decrease, or remain unchanged?
    (ii) Will the real interest rate on new loans increase, decrease, or remain unchanged?

4. Assume the nominal interest rate is 8 percent. Borrowers and lenders expect the rate of inflation to be 3 percent, and the growth rate of real GDP is 4 percent. Calculate the real interest rate.

Module 17:

Nominal vs Real Interest Rates

The difference between the nominal and real interest rates is that the real interest rate is adjusted for inflation. Interest is the cost of a loan.

Real interest rate = Nominal interest rate - inflation rate

The actual cost of borrowing is the real interest rate, not the nominal interest rate, which is simply the interest rate at face value that you would see advertised by banks.

Example: A family that A family that owns a grocery store borrows $20,000 at 5 percent nominal interest, which means they have to repay $21,000 at the end of the year. Let's say prices rise by 5 percent during that year, then the real interest rate is 0 percent. This is because when that $21,000 is paid back a year later, it has the same purchasing power as the $20,000 a year before given the 5 percent rise in prices.

The expected inflation rate is used by banks in the absence of the ability to predict exactly what inflation will be. Banks make assumptions and guesses on the level of inflation in the coming years and adjust the interest rate to take this expected inflation into account.

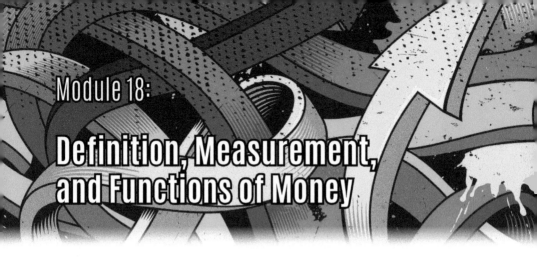

Module 18:

Definition, Measurement, and Functions of Money

Barter:

Before coins and cash money, and gold etc. were used as a means of payment, people used the barter system. Barter is the simple trade of one good for another, without using money. It was inconvenient and difficult to find someone however, who wanted the goods or services you have to offer in exchange for a good or service they have. For barter to work, you needed a double coincidence of wants and mutual agreement on the values of the exchanged goods.

Money is any asset that can be accepted as a means of payment. Money has three main functions:

○ **Medium of exchange:** Money can be used to purchase something and facilitate a transaction. For example, a $10 bill can be exchanged for a T-shirt at the store.

- **Unit of account:** Money has the ability to represent an item's value, like a new pair of headphones that cost $50.
- **Store of value:** Money can hold its value in the future. My $8 can be saved today and buy an $8 sandwich next week.

Measurements of the money supply are called M1 and M2

- M1 includes only currency in circulation (cash), travelers checks, and checkable bank deposits. They carry out transactions directly; they are the more liquid form.
- M2 includes M1 and near-moneys, or financial assets that cannot be directly used for payment, such as savings accounts. They are not as liquid as M1.
- The monetary base (M0 or MB) includes currency in circulation and bank reserves.

Calculations

M1 = Cash in circulation + travelers checks + checkable bank deposits

M2 = M1 + savings accounts + money market funds + certificates of deposit + other time deposits

MB = Cash in circulation + bank reserves

Questions

1. The transaction demand for money is very closely associated with money's use as a

    (A) store of value.
    (B) standard unit of account.
    (C) measure of value.
    (D) medium of exchange.
    (E) standard of deferred payment.

2. A barter economy is different from a money economy in that a barter economy

    (A) encourages specialization and division of labor.
    (B) involves higher costs for each transaction.
    (C) eliminates the need for a double coincidence of wants.
    (D) has only a few assets that serve as a medium of exchange.
    (E) promotes market exchanges.

3. In the narrowest definition of money, M1, or savings accounts, are excluded because they are

    (A) not a medium of exchange.
    (B) not insured by federal deposit insurance.
    (C) available from financial institutions other than banks.
    (D) a store of purchasing power.
    (E) interest-paying accounts.

4. The money demanded for the purpose of purchasing goods and services is known as

    (A) an asset demand.
    (B) a derived demand.
    (C) excess reserves.
    (D) a transactions demand.
    (E) balance of payments.

Module 19:

Banking and the Expansion of the Money Supply

How do banks create money?

When you deposit money in your bank account, that money is considered something owed by the bank, since whenever you want to, you can go to your bank and retrieve the money. This obligation to repay is referred to as a liability.

Balance sheets are what banks, other businesses, and even individuals use to summarize what they own of value and what they owe. Liabilities are on one side of the balance sheet reflecting the things you owe. On the other side are assets, or things you own. For banks, any money that is lent is considered an asset, since it is money owed to the bank that they intend to receive in the future.

Balance Sheet Example

When someone deposits $300 into the bank, assuming there was previously no money in the account, this is what the bank's balance sheet would look like:

ASSETS	LIABILITIES
$300	$300

Banks create money by using the deposits they receive (their liabilities) and lending it out. This is risky, however, since depositors can come at any time to withdraw their funds. In the unlikely event that all depositors seek to retrieve their money at the same time, the bank would fail.

To help solve this problem, banks are required to maintain a percentage of the money they receive in deposits to satisfy any deposit withdrawal. This is called the **required reserve ratio.** The bank is allowed by law to lend out the rest of the money, called excess reserves. When the bank lends money to borrowers that effectively belongs to someone else who can claim that money at any time, the bank is creating money. This process is called the **fractional reserve banking system.**

If the required reserve ratio is 10 percent, the bank would then lend out the rest and the balance sheet would look like this:

ASSETS		LIABILITIES
Reserve	$30	$300
Loans	$270	

The act of lending out money that *belongs* to others effectively increases the size of the money supply. There is more money overall since the depositors are no less well off than they were before their money was lent out by the bank; those deposits remain as assets on the depositors' balance sheets.

The Money Multiplier

The size of the expansion of the money supply after a new deposit enters the banking system depends on the money multiplier. The money multiplier explains how the maximum amount the money supply will change as a result of new money introduced to the banking system.

You can calculate the money multiplier using the following formula:

MM: Money supply
rr: Required reserve ratio

$$MM = 1/rr$$

You use the money multiplier by literally multiplying it to whatever new spending occurs, in order to see the actual impact of the spending. The money multiplier may overstate the impact of new deposits on the money supply as it does not account for:

- banks that may want to hold more excess reserves than required.
- individuals who may not deposit their money in bank accounts and hold it in cash.

A run on the bank occurs when individuals with savings in a bank no longer believe that the bank will be liquid enough to return the money if needed. This was common place during the Great Depression of the 1930's when many banks went under; lines for several blocks would form, with customers anxiously awaiting their turn to hopefully withdraw their savings. The government protects against this through depositor insurance, which guarantees up to a certain amount of money per bank account.

Questions

1. In Country Z, the required reserve ratio is 10 percent. Assume the central bank sells $50 million in government securities on the open market. Calculate each of the following.

    (i) The total change in reserves in the banking system
    (ii) The maximum possible change in the money supply

2. The central bank of the country of Sewell sells bonds on the open market. Assume that banks in Sewell have no excess reserves. What is the effect of the central bank's action on the amount of customer loans that banks in Sewell can make?

3. Assume the required reserve ratio is 10 percent. Banks keep no excess reserves, and borrowers deposit all loans made by banks. Suppose you have saved $100 in cash at home and decide to deposit it in your checking account. As a result of your deposit, the money supply can increase by a maximum of

(A) $800.
(B) $900.
(C) $1,000.
(D) $1,100.
(E) $1,200.

4. Which of the following is a determinant of the amount of money the commercial banking system can create?

(A) The marginal propensity to consume
(B) The marginal propensity to save
(C) The total number of banks
(D) The size of the federal debt
(E) The reserve requirement

5. If the reserve requirement is 10 percent and the central bank sells $10,000 in government bonds on the open market, the money supply will

(A) increase by a maximum of $9,000.
(B) increase by a maximum of $90,000.
(C) decrease by a maximum of $9,000.
(D) decrease by a maximum of $10,000.
(E) decrease by a maximum of $100,000

6. The Federal Reserve can influence the supply of money. Assume the Federal Reserve buys government bonds from commercial banks. Based on only this transaction, will the level of required reserves in the commercial banks increase, decrease, or remain the same?

7. Another monetary policy action involves changing the discount rate. Define the discount rate.

Module 20:
The Money Market

The money market is the supply and demand of highly liquid assets (cash, checks, and checking accounts) in a nation's economy. The **demand for money** refers to the amount of liquid assets like cash is desired. There is an inverse relationship between the quantity of money people want to hold, and the *nominal interest rate*. This inverse relation creates a downward slope that is the money demand curve (MD). If the interest rate is high, the opportunity cost of holding money is also high, so individuals' demand for it decreases. They are better off earning money by placing their cash in a bank deposit, since their deposit earns interest. At low nominal interest rates, holding money in a bank account is less attractive, and individuals may decide to keep more money in cash to handle everyday expenses that require it.

The supply of money is vertical as it does not depend on the interest rate. This is because it is controlled by a nation's central bank, which decides the supply by taking actions or implementing monetary policy. In the United States, this is institution is called the Federal Reserve. In Canada it is the Bank of Canada.

When the interest rate at which the quantity of money demanded is equal to the quantity of money supplied, we get the money market equilibrium.

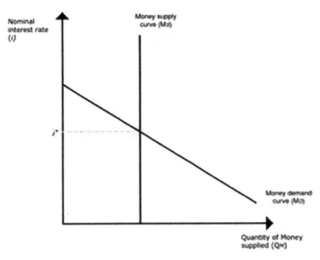

Figure 20.1

Changes in the Money Market

Certain factors can cause changes in the money demand: the price level, monetary policy, changes in GDP, and technology. If the demand for money increases at any given interest rate, the demand curve shifts to the right (a decrease shifts it to the left). Such a shift creates disequilibrium interest rates and shortages/surpluses in the money market. The interest rate always adjusts and brings the money supply to a level that will remain at equilibrium.

It is important to note that bond prices and interest rates are also inversely related. People want to hold less money if there is a higher interest rate on bonds and other investments.

Gross Domestic Product

As GDP has steadily increased in Canada, so has money demand. This is an example of a shift in demand as consumers want to spend more money when the economy is growing.

Figure 20.2

Figure 20.2 illustrates both the increase and decrease of the money supply curve. If there is an increase in the money supply (MS2), the interest rate will fall until it reaches i2 and establishes a new equilibrium in the money market.

Questions

1. In Country Z, the required reserve ratio is 10 percent. Assume the central bank sells $50million in government securities on the open market. Using a correctly labeled graph of the money market, show the impact of the central bank's bond sale on the nominal interest rate.

2. An increase in inflationary expectations most likely affects nominal interest rates and bond prices in which of the following ways in the short run?

    Nominal Interest, Rates Bond Prices
    (A) Increase, No change
    (B) Increase, Decrease
    (C) No change, Increase
    (D) Decrease, Increase
    (E) Decrease, Decrease

Module 21:
Monetary Policy

As you have learned, the central bank controls the supply of money in the money market. Monetary policy is one of the ways it can do this. There are two types of these policies among three different tools, all used while maintaining the central bank's overall goal of controlling inflation, reducing unemployment, and managing moderate long-term interest rates.

Open Market Operations

The first and most common strategy is **open market operations**, which is the sale or purchase by the central bank of government debt such as short-term bonds known as *treasury bills*. When the central bank sells the bonds, the money supply in the economy decreases. When bonds are purchased by the central bank from different institutions and businesses, the money supply increases. It also important to note that open market operations have a larger impact on the money supply than just the increase in monetary base due to the money multiplier.

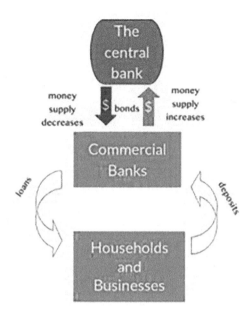

Reserve Ratio

Another monetary policy is the **reserve ratio**. This is the percentage of money commercial banks in the nation must hold in their reserves instead of having it lent out in the economy. If the central bank chooses a lower reserve ratio to be met, commercial banks can lend more money, meaning a higher money supply in the economy through the money multiplier (refer to Module 23). If the reserve ratio is increased to a higher percentage, banks must lend out less money, therefore causing a restriction on liquidity and a decrease in the money supply.

Discount Rate

The third and less common monetary policy strategy is the **discount rate**. This is the interest rate charged to banks for borrowing funds from the central bank. When the discount rate is increased to a higher percentage, commercial banks are discouraged from borrowing from the central bank, and there is a decrease in money supply. A decrease in the discount rate, however, means a higher supply of money to encourage borrowing and growth in the economy.

Overnight Interbank Lending

The overnight rate is the interest rate that large banks use to borrow and lend from one another in the short-term. They do these loans overnight using open market operations to meet the reserve requirement for the following day.

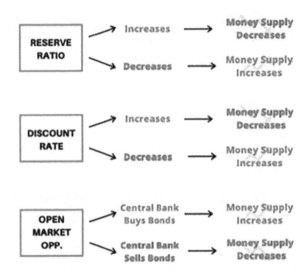

Types of Monetary Policy

Contractionary monetary policy is used to reduce inflation by restricting money banks can lend. This type of policy aims at having individuals borrow less money, therefore slowing growth and the money supply.

Expansionary monetary policy is used to boost the economy by increasing the amount of money available to banks to lend. The aim is to lower interest rates to increase the demand and supply for money so consumers want to purchase more.

Contractionary Actions:
- Selling government bonds
- increasing the reserve ratio
- increasing the discount rate

Expansionary Actions:
- Buying government bonds
- Reducing the reserve ratio

*Reducing the discount rate

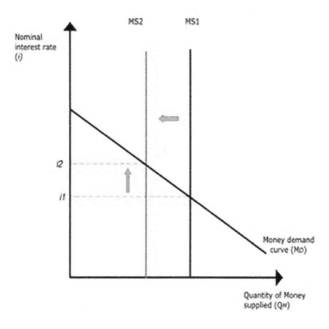

Figure 21.1

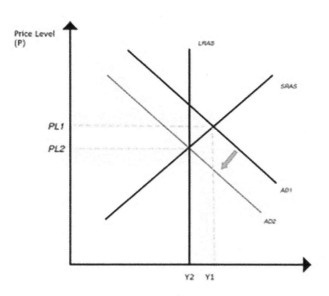

Figure 21.2

Tip: Be able to line up Figure 21.1 and 21.2 in your answers.

The money market model and the AD-AS model can be used to demonstrate the short-run effects of a monetary policy. Let's say the government wants to reduce an inflationary gap and raises the reserve requirement. A higher reserve requirement would reduce the money supply as shown in figure 22.3 because it would mean that banks lend less. If banks lend less, reducing the money supply -Aggregate Demand will fall as shown in Figure 22.4, shifting the AD curve back to the long run equilibrium point.

Questions

1. Which of the following will lead to a decrease in a nation's money supply?

    (A) A decrease in income tax rates
    (B) A decrease in the discount rate
    (C) An open market purchase of government securities by the central bank
    (D) An increase in reserve requirements
    (E) An increase in government expenditures on goods and services

2. If a country's economy is operating below the full-employment level of output at a very low inflation rate, the central bank of the country is most likely to:

    (A) pursue an expansionary monetary policy because it is required to do so by law whenever output is below the full employment level.
    (B) pursue an expansionary fiscal policy because it is required to do so by law whenever output is below the full employment level.
    (C) lower the discount rate and buy bonds on the open market to generate an increase in output.
    (D) lower the required reserve ratio and sell bonds on the open market to generate an increase in output.
    (E) raise the discount rate and lower the required reserve ratio to generate an increase in output.

3. For which of the following sets of unemployment and inflation rates will a central bank be most reluctant to increase the rate of growth in the money supply?

    Unemployment Rate, Inflation Rate
    (A) 10 percent, 2 percent
    (B) 10 percent, 5 percent
    (C) 10 percent, 10 percent
    (D) 5 percent, 5 percent
    (E) 5 percent, 10 percent

4. Advocates of a monetary rule recommend increasing the money supply at a rate equal to the rate of increase in which of the following?

(A) Price level
(B) Unemployment rate
(C) Level of exports
(D) Level of imports
(E) Long-run real gross domestic product

5. Assume the country of Uikenland is in an economic peak, and experiencing an inflationary gap. Also assume the Central Bank of Rankinland pursues a contractionary monetary policy.

(i)   Identify the open-market operation the Central Bank would use.
(ii) Draw a correctly labeled money market graph and show the short-run effect of the contractionary monetary policy on the nominal interest rate.
(iii) Assuming no change to the price level, what happens to the real interest rate as a result of the contractionary monetary policy? Explain.
(iv) Given your answer to part (iii) regarding the real interest rate, what happens to the real GDP in the short run? Explain.

6. Which of the following will lower the prices of a country's outstanding government bonds?

(A) An open-market purchase of government bonds by the country's central bank
(B) A decrease in the required reserve ratio for the country's commercial banks
(C) An outflow of financial capital to other countries
(D) A decrease in the country's government spending
(E) A decrease in inflationary expectations in the country

Module 22:

The Loanable Funds Market

The loanable funds market is a hypothetical model between borrowers and savers in an economy. The *real interest rate* (nominal interest rate − inflation rate) shows the price of a loan, which tells you the return for lenders and the price borrowers have to pay for the service of getting a loan funds in the market. In this example we assume there is just one type of interest rate.

The demand of loanable funds curve shows the willingness to borrow money, and the supply of loanable funds curve shows the willingness to save money.

Remember from the module on banking that the savings we put into banks becomes money they can lend to others; hence our savings can be considered the supply of loanable funds.

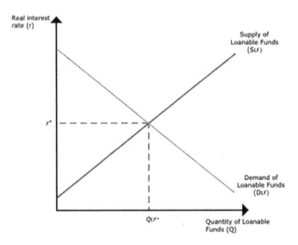

Figure 22.1

As shown in Figure 22.1 the real interest rate and the quantity supplied of loanable funds increase together. The real interest rate and the quantity demanded of loanable funds have a negative correlation relationship.

This is because when the interest rate is low, individuals are eager to get a loan. However, not many lenders want to loan money at such a low rate since they can make money investing it elsewhere.

The profit made from a loan is called the rate of return. We get an equilibrium in the loanable funds market when the real interest rate is such that the quantities demanded and supplied of loanable funds are equal.

Changes in Supply and Demand

The determinants in changes to the demand in a loanable funds market depend on the investment demand, such as:

- The rate of return earned on investing in a project
- Government policies, like an investment tax credit

The determinants in changes to the supply in a loanable funds market depend on saving behaviors, such as:

- Changes in capital inflows, for example less income or GDP
- Changes in savings behavior, like the need to save more due to a fear of a recession
- Changes in public savings, for example a government increase in budget surplus

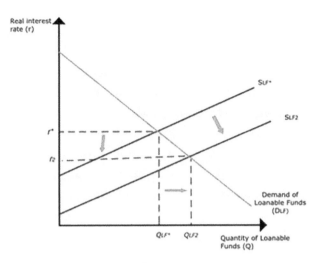

Figure 22.2

National Savings in an Economy

We can use the savings and lending model in our GDP equation to further define savings on a national level. First we will focus on a *closed economy*, where there is no international borrowing or lending.

We know **GDP = Y**
where Y denotes national income

Y= C + I + G = Consumption + **I**nvestment + **G**overnment Spending
If we want to subtract consumption and government spending from national income, we end up with:

Y - C - G = I
Y- C - G equates to national savings (S) in a closed economy

S=I

Therefore, national savings are equal to investment, as money saved is being invested. This is also the total amount of private savings and public savings. How so? If we add taxes to the equation, we get:
Y - T- C + T - G = I

This can be broken down into public savings: **T - G**
And private savings: **Y- C-T**

How does the model change with an open economy?

An open economy allows for trade and overseas investments, so it includes net capital inflows (NCI).

The model then becomes:

Y= C + I + G + NCI

Y - T - C + T - G + NCI = I

Questions

1. Japan, the European Union, Canada, and Mexico have flexible exchange rates. Suppose Japan attracts an increased amount of investment from the European Union.

    (i)   Using a correctly labeled graph of the loanable funds market in Japan, show the effect of the increase in foreign investment on the real interest rate in Japan.
    (ii) How will the real interest rate change in Japan identified in part (i) affect the employment level in Japan in the short run? Explain.

2. Assume that as a result of increased political instability, investors move their funds out of the country of Tara. Using a correctly labeled graph of the loanable funds market, show the impact of this decision by investors on the real interest rate.

Module 23:

Fiscal and Monetary Policy Actions in the Short Run

Now that you have learned about both monetary and fiscal policy and how they are used separately to create equilibrium in the economy, you can combine them to see their effects when used simultaneously.

As a quick reminder, fiscal policy is made by the government and focuses on taxes and government spending. Monetary policy is made by the central bank and focuses on the supply of money.

Using Expansionary Policies (Increasing Output)

If there is high unemployment and a negative output gap (PL1 and Y1), both institutions will use their expansionary policies. The government may choose to cut taxes, which will shift the AD to the right. Similarly, the central bank will put in place a policy to increase the money supply, for example a lower reserve ratio. Together, by pushing the price level up to P2 and output right to Y2, AD will shift to the right until it reaches the equilibrium.

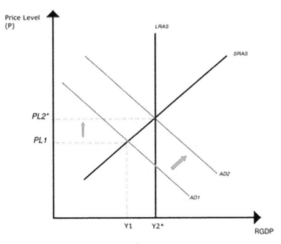

Figure 23.1

Using Contractionary Policies (Decreasing Output)

In certain cases, the economy may be expanding too much, resulting in high inflation rates and a disequilibrium in terms of surplus (Y1 and PL1). Contractionary fiscal and monetary policies can be combined to decrease the money supply and slow economic growth. For the fiscal policy, the government may choose to directly decrease its spending. The central bank will want to decrease the money supply perhaps by selling treasury bills. Both of these policies will cause the AD curve to shift to the left by lowering the price level and output until they return to equilibrium. The reason AD falls is because these policies pull money out of the economic system.

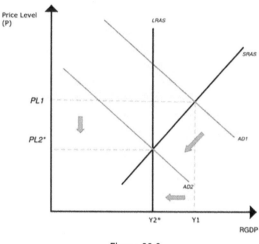

Figure 23.2

Policy Lags

A policy lag is the time between when a problem arises in the economy and the effect of the policy actually starting to work. This delay impacts both monetary and fiscal policies. It can happen due to four main types of lags:

- Data lag: A delay due to the efforts it takes to get the proper macroeconomic data for addressing an issue. It can be difficult to gather accurate data about the economy, and time is needed for research and revision.
- Recognition lag: The initial time it takes to recognize the problem happening in the economy. For example, unemployment could be on the rise, but authorities will not notice immediately because of reporting and data.

- Decision or legislative lag: The delay caused by the time it takes to decide on how to handle the economic problem at hand. This is due to authorities having to deliberate, vote, and go through a process to pick the best course of action.
- Implementation lag: The time it takes to actually implement the policy; for example, setting up or informing the proper institutions and making a budget.
- Effectiveness lag: Even once the policy is recognized, chosen, and implemented, there is still a delay from when the policy is put into place to when it becomes effective in the economy. Monetary policy suffers from this lag more than fiscal policy.

Questions

1. In the short run, an expansionary monetary policy will most likely result in which of the following changes in the price level and real GDP?

Price Level | Real GDP
(A) Decrease | Increase
(B) No change | Decrease
(C) Increase | No change
(D) Increase | Decrease
(E) Increase | Increase

2. A reduction in inflation can best be achieved by which of the following combinations of fiscal and monetary policy?

Fiscal Policy | Monetary Policy
(A) Increase taxes | Sell government bonds
(B) Decrease taxes | Buy government bonds
(C) Decrease taxes | Lower margin requirements
(D) Decrease government spending | Lower discount rate spending
(E) Increase government spending | Raise discount rate spending

3. A discretionary fiscal policy action to reduce inflation in the short run would be to:

(A) increase transfer payments to those on fixed incomes.
(B) increase taxes or decrease government spending.
(C) decrease taxes or increase government spending.
(D) increase taxes and the money supply.
(E) decrease taxes and interest rates.

4. With an upward-sloping AS curve, an increase in the money supply will affect the price level and real GDP in the short run in which of the following ways?

Price Level | Real GDP
(A) Decrease | Decrease
(B) Decrease | Increase
(C) Increase | Decrease
(D) Increase | Increase
(E) No change | No change

Named after Alban W. H. Phillips in the late 1900s, the Phillips curve shows the inverse relationship between inflation and unemployment. It is modeled by putting the rate of inflation on the vertical axis and the rate of unemployment on the horizontal axis.

When there is high inflation, there is low unemployment, and vise-versa. This trade-off is therefore downward sloping and relevant only in the short-run; hence, it is modeled by the short-run Phillips curve (SRPC). This relationship does not hold in the long-run. As shown in Figure 24.1 the long-run Phillips curve (LRPC) is vertical at the natural rate of unemployment. This is the unemployment rate unaffected by business cycle movement like recessions.

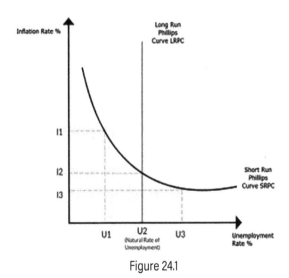

Figure 24.1

At any given moment, the economy can be in:

- recession (U3, I3), or at any point on the SRPC to the right of the LRPC.
- equilibrium or full employment (U2, I2), where SRPC = LRPC.
- an inflationary gap (U1, I1), or any point on the SRPH to the left of the LRPC.

How does the Phillips curve respond to changes in demand and supply?

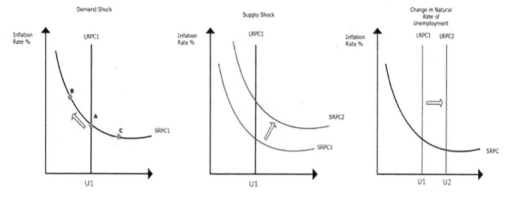

Figure 24.2

1. Left Image: When the economy is in long-run equilibrium, and it experiences an AD shock, there is a shift along the SRPC. If there is an increase, it will move from point A to point B, and a decrease in supply would cause a movement from point A to C. It would then adjust in the long run to point A.

2. Middle Image: When short-run AS is affected, the SRPC shifts in the opposite direction of the supply increase or decrease. In this example, the supply decreases, and the SRPC shifts up to the right. If supply increases, the SRPC shifts to the left.

3. In Figure 25.2, the Right Image shows a shift in the LRPC. Anything that affects the natural rate of unemployment (frictional + structural unemployment) move the LRPC to the left or right.

Questions

1. Assume the economy of Country X has an actual unemployment rate of 7 percent, a natural rate of unemployment of 5 percent, and an inflation rate of 3 percent. Assume the government takes no policy action to reduce unemployment.

In the long run, will each of the following shift to the right, shift to the left, or remain the same?

(i) Short-run AS curve. Explain.
(ii) LRPC

Module 25:

Money Growth and Inflation

How are inflation and the money supply related? An increase in the money supply leads to an increase in AD on our AD-AS model. If we start at the equilibrium point A and increase the money supply, AD increases to AD2. We would be at a new output level, Y2, and a higher price level, P2, shown by point B. However, this is for only a short period of time; in the long run, the economy will return to the LRAS equilibrium along the demand curve or point C. It is now at a higher price level, P3, but at the same level of output, Y1, leaving us with inflation.

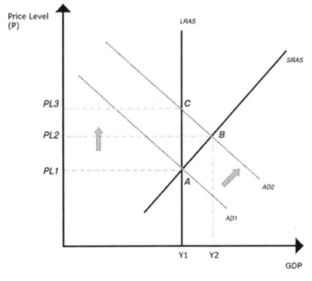

Figure 25.1

By printing more money and increasing the supply, the AD for goods increases, as households have more money. If there is more money for the same amount of goods, firms increase prices. This means more expensive goods at the same amount of output or inflation.

90

Zimbabwe

Zimbabwe found itself in a situation of hyperinflation. Starting in the 1990s the country had sharp falls in output while having high government debt. As its output level continued to fall, the government decided to print money to pay off debt and increase output to avoid a large recession. This increase of money supply led to hyperinflation. In November 2008 there was an estimated 79,600,000,000 percent in inflation. Zimbabwe's currency is no longer used because of high inflation, and the country has switched to US dollars.

Quantity Theory of Money

The quantity theory of money states that any increase in the money supply causes an increase in the price level, when the velocity of money is fixed and output is at full employment output.

Equation: $M \times V = P \times Y$

where:
M = Money supply
Y= Output (real GDP)
P= Price level
V= Velocity of money

The velocity of money (V) describes how many times a dollar circulates in the economy. In the quantity theory of money we treat it as fixed, as it does not fluctuate much in the short run.

If we were to calculate for *velocity* with the following values, we could rearrange our equation:

$M = 100$
$Y = 200$
$P = 1.4$

$V = P \times Y/M$
$V = 2.8$

Module 26:
Government Deficits and the National Debt

As you have learned, the government is responsible for fiscal policy and can use expansionary measures to help grow the economy and decrease unemployment. However, it cannot always do things like decrease taxes or increase its expenditure, as it is on a budget that depends on how much revenue and spending it does in a year, like any business or person.

The **budget deficit** is when spending and transfer payments exceed the government's tax revenue in a given year. When this happens, the government must borrow that money as a loan. The accumulation of such debt is known as **national** or **public debt**. The government can also experience a **budget surplus**, when the tax income is higher than what was spent during the year.

We can calculate if the government is experiencing a deficit or surplus by finding government savings:

Government savings = Tax revenue − government spending

For example:

	2017	2018	2019
Government saving	-$200	-$200	+$400
Debt	$200	$400	$0

- Let's say in 2017 the government has $800 of revenue but spends $1,000. It will run a deficit and debt of $200 (assuming it had no debt before).
- In 2018 it once again runs a deficit of $200. This adds to an accumulated total debt of $400.

- If the following year, in 2019, it cuts down how much it spends and runs a budget surplus of $400, there is now a balanced budget, and the debt is equal to $0.

The national debt of the United States was around $22 trillion as of February 2019. How does this happen?

As a resident of a country, we benefit from deficit spending as it drives economic growth and can improve our quality of life when it is spent on things like health care and transportation. However, the accumulation of this debt can have negative long-term impacts and prevent further spending. Primarily this is due to interest rates. Therefore we can adjust our calculation for the budget to include interest in 2019.

Government savings = tax revenue - government spending - (loan + (loan x interest rate))
= 400 – (400 + (400 x .10)
= - 40

For 2019, in order for there to be a budget surplus and balanced budget, government savings would actually have to be $440, assuming a 10% interest rate.

If a country is not running any budget surpluses and the national debt continues to increase, so does the amount of interest. This can eventually get so large it becomes unsustainable and even impossible to pay just the interest off. Instead of spending any surplus on things that will benefit the nation, the government will be forced to pay back debt or incur more debt. High debt can cause interest rates to rise, which I will expand on in the next unit.

Questions

1. Assume that with a proportional tax system, the government always sets the tax rate at a level that yields a balanced budget at full employment. Which of the following is necessarily true?

   (A) The government budget will balance every year.
   (B) The government budget will be in deficit over the business cycle.
   (C) The national debt will increase in any year the economy operates below full employment.
   (D) Crowding out of private investment will occur whenever the economy operates at full employment.
   (E) The tax system destabilize.

2. Which of the following policy combinations could reduce a government deficit without changing aggregate demand?

    (A) An increase in taxes and a decrease in the money supply
    (B) An increase in taxes and an increase in the money supply
    (C) A decrease in taxes and a decrease in the money supply
    (D) A decrease in government spending and a decrease in the money supply
    (E) An increase in government spending and a decrease in the money supply

3. If the federal government decreases its expenditures on goods and services by $10 billion and decreases taxes on personal incomes by $10 billion, which of the following will occur in the short run?

    (A) The federal budget deficit will increase by $10 billion.
    (B) The federal budget deficit will decrease by $10 billion.
    (C) Aggregate income will remain the same.
    (D) Aggregate income will increase by up to $10 billion.
    (E) Aggregate income will decrease by up to $10 billion.

Module 27:

Crowding Out

One of the potential issues surrounding high government debt is the rise in interest rates, which can have a negative impact on economic growth due to crowding out. **Crowding out** is when a government borrows money and "crowds out" private-sector borrowing and investment, leading to less growth and less investment in the economy.

We can model this by returning to the loanable funds market graph (see Module 23)

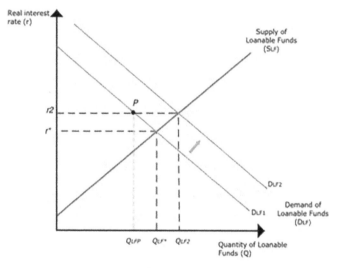

Figure 27.1

When the government has to borrow to pay its debt, it is competing with the rest of the private sector for these loanable funds. If the government needs to borrow, it increases the demand, moving the demand of loanable funds curve (DLF) to the right (DLF1 to DLF2). This moves the real interest rate, or the price of borrowing, to r2.

Assuming that before the new demand, the government was not borrowing, the demand curve DLF1 was represented by only the private sector. This would mean at a higher rate, such as r2, the interest-sensitive private sector could afford to borrow only at point P. Lower private investment in the long term can slow the rate of capital accumulation, which results in slow growth.

Long-Run Impacts of Crowding Out

Long run crowding out can cause a lower rate of physical capital accumulation and eventually less economic growth. To grow businesses or buy properties, people will borrow money. If there are high interest rates, there will be less incentive to borrow and a slow in growth of GDP.

Module 28:

Economic Growth

When economists talk, they mention the term 'economic growth' often, but what exactly is economic growth, and how do we define it?

To measure growth, focus on GDP per capita over time. It measures the total value of an economy's production of final goods and services, without the effects of rising price levels in a given year. It is then divided by the population size to avoid any effects of population changes.

A single period of positive or negative GDP levels does not define economic growth as it could just be part of the natural business cycle. Rather, we look for long-term trends in the economy when discussing growth.

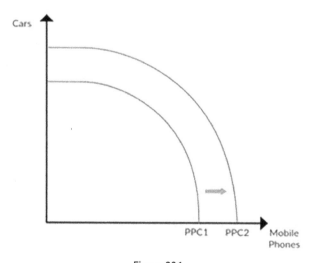

Figure 28.1

If the capacity to produce more increases, so does the PPC. What can cause this?

- Better *technology*: An invention that increases productivity, such as computer programs including the internet.
- *Improvements in human capital*: Labor productivity increases through better education or improved health
- *Improvements in physical capital*: Goods that will help, like investments in new infrastructure or equipment

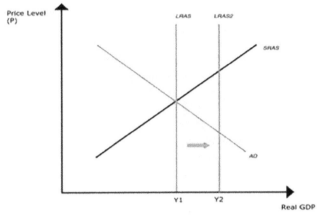

Figure 28.2

Economic growth can be depicted as the rightward shift in the PPC seen in Figure 29.1 but it can also be reflected as a rightward shift in the LRAS curve in Figure 28.2.

Aggregate Production Function

The aggregate production function is a hypothetical function that shows how productivity in terms of output per worker relies on the amount of physical capital and human capital as well as the state of technology. Output per capita is positively related to capital per capita (both human and physical capital). The function shows that if any of the factors increase or decrease, output does the same.

$$Y = A \ \boldsymbol{\times} \ (K, L) \text{ - where it is some function of K and L}$$

Example of aggregate production function: $Y = A \times K^{\alpha} L^{1-\alpha}$

$$Y = \text{Output}$$

$$A = \text{Technology (total factor productivity)}$$

K= Physical capital

L= Human capital

= variable between 0 and 1

Question

1.   Assume that as a result of increased political instability, investors move their funds out of the country of Tara, and the interest rate increases.

   (i)   What will happen to Tara's rate of economic growth? Explain.

2.   An increase in net investment leads to faster economic growth because capital per worker and output per worker will change in which of the following ways?

	Capital Output per Worker	Output per Worker
(A)	Increase	Increase
(B)	Increase	Decrease
(C)	No change	Increase
(D)	Decrease	Increase
(E)	Decrease	Decrease

Module 29:
Public Policy and Economic Growth

Economic growth differs from country to country. Public policies and government spending play an important role in determining national income and the standard of living. Policies aimed at improving productivity focus on the labor supply and in turn increase GDP per capita and economic growth.

- *Investing in human capital:* Giving more training and education to people, or having better health-care coverage makes workers more productive
- *Encouraging a higher labor force participation* means more workers for the same population size, which would increase output per capita. A good example of this is encouraging discouraged workers to look for work, by offering incentives.

Policies can increase economic growth by investing in technology and capital, which pushes the PPC outwards as there is more capacity to produce.

Investing in physical capital: Governments provide the majority of infrastructure in a country, like roads, bridges, and power supplies needed to operate economic and social activities. Regulations to maintain these are important, so when private companies build things like housing or electricity systems, they are meet health and safety standards.

Technology: Governments can provide initiatives in research and development, which is any spending on new technologies and capital growth; for example, generating loans or tax credits for the research of more efficient machinery.

Supply-Side Fiscal Policies

Supply-side fiscal policies affect AD, AS, and potential output in the short and long run. Supply-side approaches focus on increasing the supply of goods to lead to economic growth. Supply-side fiscal policies impact incentives that change business economic behavior.

For example, a corporate tax reduction gives businesses more cash to invest in their enterprise, producing more supply. Another example is decreasing business regulations, which gives incentive to more firms to appear and increase overall supply.

Questions

1. Assume that the United States economy is currently in long-run equilibrium then the real interest rate increases; what is the impact on each of the following?

    (i)   Investment
    (ii) Economic growth rate. Explain.

2. An increase in which of the following would be most likely to increase long-run growth?

    (A) Pension payments
    (B) Unemployment compensations
    (C) Subsidies to businesses for purchases of capital goods
    (D) Tariffs on imported capital goods
    (E) Tariffs on imported oil

Module 30:
Balance of Payments Accounts

The current account records transactions of merchandise, services, interest, and dividend income between one country and the rest of the world.

It specifically includes:

- net exports (X-M).
- net income from abroad (NI).
- net unilateral transfers (NT).

Current account formula: CA = (X-M) + NI + NT

The current account may be in one of three positions:

- Balanced: The same amount of money that leaves the economy is returned.
- Deficit: More money left the economy to other countries than was received.
- Surplus: An economy with a current account surplus received more money from other countries in a given period than was received.

A country's balance of trade is the same thing as net exports.

The capital and financial account records financial capital transfers and purchases or sales of assets between countries. It includes financial assets (stocks, bonds, etc.) and direct foreign investment (businesses, real estate).

A surplus in the capital and financial account means there has been a net inflow of financial capital. A deficit in the capital and financial account means there has been a net outflow of financial capital. It can also be balanced.

Balance of Payments, Defined:

The balance of payments is an accounting system that records a country's international transactions. The current account and the capital and financial account make up the balance of payments.

Transactions that cause money to flow into an economy are a positive or credit to that country's balance of payments. Any transaction that causes money to flow out is a debit.

The sum of all credit transactions must equal the sum of all debit transactions (CA+CFA=0). When they do not balance, the central bank must buy or sell currency in order to balance it.

The full balance of payments is CA + CFA +Δ official reserves = 0.

Current account surpluses must be offset by financial account deficits. Current account deficits must be offset by financial account surpluses.

All balance of payments transactions impact the foreign currency markets. When an American purchases a good from Canada, the American must demand Canadian dollars and supply US dollars in exchange. All else being equal, this reduces the value of US dollars and increases the value of Canadian dollars.

Capital inflows such as direct investment from another country or purchases of stocks and bonds from another country and central bank purchases of assets increase the supply of loanable funds; capital outflows decrease the supply of loanable funds.

Questions

1. United States firm sells $10 million worth of goods to a firm in Argentina, where the currency is the peso. Assume that the United States current account balance with Argentina is initially zero. How will the transaction above affect the United States current account balance? Explain.

2. A country can have an increased surplus in its balance of trade as a result of

    (A) an increase in domestic inflation
    (B) declining imports and rising exports
    (C) higher tariffs imposed by its trading partners
    (D) an increase in capital inflow
    (E) an appreciating currency

3. Which of the following is true in the short run if consumers buy more imported goods and fewer domestic goods?

    (A) The trade balance moves toward deficit, and equilibrium income decreases.
    (B) The trade balance moves toward deficit, and equilibrium income increases.
    (C) The trade balance moves toward surplus, and equilibrium income is unaffected.
    (D) The trade balance moves toward surplus, and equilibrium income decreases.
    (E) The trade balance is unaffected, and equilibrium income decreases.

4. The European Union and the United States are trading partners. If the current account balance is zero, will an increase in United States real income result in a current account surplus, deficit, or no change? Explain.

Module 31:

Exchange Rates

An **exchange rate** is the value of a country's currency in terms of the currency of another country. For example when talking about the exchange rate of the U.S Dollar you would analyze how many Canadian dollars you can receive for one U.S Dollar -> CAD/USD

Exchange rate for currency A = unit of currency B/unit of currency A

The demand and supply of a currency impacts that currency's exchange rate or relative value of one country's currency to another. When an American buys a Chinese good, the United States supplies the US dollar while demanding Chinese yuan in order to make the purchase.

Determinants that can shift supply and demand of currency:

1. Tastes and preferences of goods and services in another country (For example, Korean K-Pop has become very popular, boosting demand for Korean K-Pop related goods and services, which would require the purchase of South Korean won.)

2. Price Level: higher price levels depresses demand from other countries.

3. Income: higher income creates higher demand for foreign goods and services.

4. Interest Rates: explained in Module 33

This is why the exchange rate is always fluctuating, as we will see in the following unit about the foreign exchange market. A nation's currency can either:

-   Appreciate: Gain value and exchange rate becomes stronger or higher.
-   Depreciate: Lose value and exchange rate becomes weaker or lower.

How do you calculate the value of one exchange rate in relation to another? If the US dollar/Chinese yuan exchange rate is 10, it means it costs 10 Chinese yuans to purchase 1 US dollar. However, if we are looking at the yuan/dollar exchange rate, we can use the formula: 1/exchange rate. In this case, 1 / 10 = 0.10. It costs 0.10 US dollars to buy a Chinese yuan.

If the US dollar/Chinese yuan exchange rate increases to 11, it would now cost [1/11=0.9] or 9 cents in US dollars to buy one Chinese yuan. The US Dollar in this case has appreciated.

If the exchange rate dropped to 9, it would now cost more [1/9=.11 or 11 cents] to buy one Chinese yuan; depreciation of the US dollar.

Exchange rates and interest rates are important for macroeconomic decision making.

Question:

1. Assume that yesterday the exchange rate between the euro and the Singaporean dollar was 1 euro = 0.58 Singaporean dollars. Assume that today the euro is trading at 1 euro = 0.60 Singaporean dollars. How will the change in the exchange rate affect each of the following in Singapore in the short run?

    (i)   Aggregate demand. Explain.
    (ii) The level of employment. Explain.

Module 32:
The Foreign Exchange Market

Just as we trade stocks and bonds on the stock market, we can trade currencies on a global decentralized market called the **foreign exchange market**.

The foreign exchange market is a virtual market where the trade of currencies take place:

It:

- Underpins trade: People use their country's currency (e.g., euros) to buy goods and services from another country and the foreign exchange market facilitates trade from home currency to foreign currency in order to make a purchase.
- Underpins investment: People use their home currency to purchase assets such as stocks, bonds, or real estate from another country, and the foreign exchange market trades one currency for another to facilitate the purchase.

The relationship between the supply and demand of a currency is inverse, as modeled below. For this example I will model the foreign exchange market for the British pound (GBP). The horizontal axis is the quantity of the currency in the market. The vertical axis is the price of the currency, called the **exchange rate**. The exchange rate is shown in terms of another currency, which in this example is the amount of US dollars per British pound.

The demand curve is downward sloping. When the exchange rate is high, the quantity demanded is low. Less people in the United States will want to purchase the British pound at such a high exchange rate compared to their currency.

The supply of currency is upward sloping. As the exchange rate increases, the currency becomes more valuable, making foreign goods/assets/services relatively cheap, which increases the amount of local currency supplied in order to purchase foreign goods. The equilibrium exchange rate at e* and Q* is the point at which the quantity of the British pound is equal to the supply.

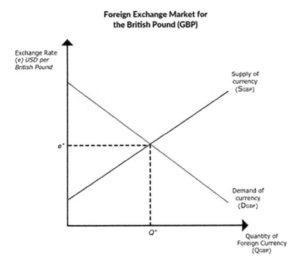

Figure 32.1

Currencies can appreciate or depreciate, meaning they are gaining or losing value. Things like major macroeconomic events, current account deficits, trade policy, and monetary policy play a huge role in the foreign exchange market.

For example, if the United Kingdom decided to increase exports due to a new trade regulation, more currency will be demanded by foreign nations to purchase these exports. This will shift the demand curve to the right. As quantity increases, it will create a disequilibrium surplus in the market. The exchange rate will increase from e1 to e2, appreciating the British pound and decreasing quantity to arrive back at the equilibrium exchange rate.

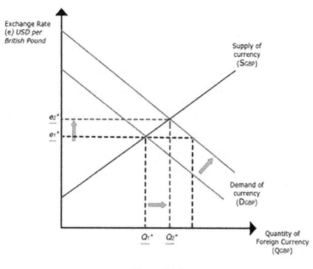

Figure 32.2

It is important to note that the US dollar would have a mirrored foreign exchange if talking about the British pound. As the British pound appreciates relative to the US dollar, the US dollar is depreciating relative to the pound. In this lesson we focused on only the floating exchange rate, which is the rate determined by the supply and demand in the open market. Most major nations have this type of exchange rate to determine their currency's value. There is also the fixed exchange rate, which is determined and set by a government's monetary authority. It links the country's rate to another more stable currency or measure to provide more certainty, less fluctuation, and lower inflation. For example, The Bahamas tied its dollar to the US dollar at a rate of 1 to 1.

Purchasing Power Parity

Purchasing power parity (PPP) is another method of comparing countries' currencies through a common basket of goods. It calculates how much something would cost all around the world in terms of the US dollars. It can be used to find the most expensive and cheapest countries to purchase a good in.

Exchange rate of currency A = Cost of basket in currency A/ cost of basket in currency B

Question:

1.   A United States firm sells $10 million worth of goods to a firm in Argentina, where the currency is the peso. Using a correctly labeled graph of the foreign exchange market

for the United States dollar, show how a decrease in the United States financial investment in Argentina affects each of the following.

(i) The supply of United States dollars

(ii) The value of the United States dollar relative to the peso

2. The value of a country's currency will tend to appreciate if

(A) demand for the country's exports increases

(B) the country's money supply increases

(C) the country's citizens increase their travel abroad

(D) domestic interest rates decrease

(E) tariffs on the country's imports decrease

3. Which of the following is most likely to benefit from an appreciation in the United States dollar in the short run?

(A) United States investors holding European bonds

(B) Importers in foreign countries seeking raw inputs at a lower price

(C) United States exporters selling capital equipment

(D) United States tourists traveling to foreign countries

(E) European consumers buying United States goods

Module 33:

Effect of Changes in Policies and Economic Conditions on the Foreign Exchange Market

Changes in the supply and demand of a currency cause it to appreciate or depreciate in a flexible exchange market. This influences the flow of goods, services, and financial capital between countries. Factors that change the demand of a currency are preferences, interest rates, expected future exchange rates, price levels and the national income.

Factors that influence the supply of a currency are based on the demand of another currency. When a foreign currency is demanded, it must be supplied (purchased) by the domestic buyers' currency. So if you live in the United States and have US dollars, you will increase the supply of US dollars when you need to purchase Chinese yuan.

Let's see the effects of each determinate on the demand of a currency and as a result the supply of another. We will be using the United States and Poland as examples:

Preferences

Demand: A country's exports can increase or decrease if consumers from other countries change their tastes and preferences for the good. If a popular movie comes out that popularizes oranges from Florida, the US, it will make the Polish want to buy more oranges and import them to Poland. Therefore, the demand for US dollars increases and it appreciates.

Supply: If the demand for US dollars increases, the supply of Polish zloty (PLN) decreases, causing it to depreciate.

Interest Rates

If the interest rates in the United States rises to 8 percent, and it is only 5 percent in Poland, Polish investors will want to buy US assets to take advantage of the higher interest rate, and will need more US dollars, increasing the demand and appreciating the value of the dollar. Since the demand for US dollars increases, the supply of PLN increases. This causes the PLN to depreciate.

Expected Future Exchange Rates

If investors think there may be an increase or decrease in a currency or asset in a nation in the future, this can impact the desire for it. If there is a political problem happening in the United States that may impact investments and the amount of risk, Poland investors will no longer want US assets. The demand for US dollars will decrease, and it will depreciate.

The supply of the PLN will decrease and therefore appreciate.

Price Level

When price levels are lower in a country, goods and services are demanded more. If inflation is lower at 4 percent in the United States than 9 percent in Poland, Poland will want to buy more goods in US dollars, increasing the demand. This will appreciate the dollar.

The supply of PLN increases to purchase more US dollars, and the PLN depreciates.

National Income

Higher national income leads to a higher demand of foreign goods. If Poland experiences a sharp increase in GDP, there will be a higher demand for US cars, increasing demand and appreciating the US dollar.

Once again the demand for US dollars increases, so the PLN supply increases and the value depreciates.

Tariffs and Quotas

The supply of a currency is directly influenced by tariffs and quotas.

Tariff

A tariff is a tax placed on imported goods into a nation. If Poland placed a tariff on foreign goods, the supply of the PLN would decrease as there is less of a need to purchase foreign goods and currency. This would cause it to appreciate.

Quota

A quota is a limit placed by the government on the amount of goods allowed to be imported. If Poland put a quota on foreign goods coming into Poland, it would have the same effect as a tariff: less purchasing of imports, a decrease in the supply of PLN, and appreciation of the PLN.

US Dollar (USD) appreciating due to an increase in USD demand:

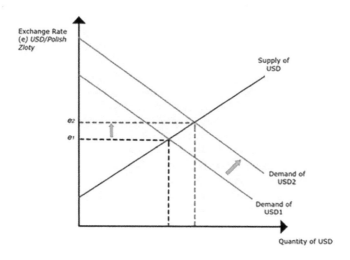

Figure 33.1

Zloty (PLN) depreciating due to an increase in supply of Zloty:

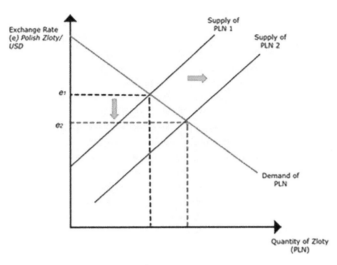

Figure 33.2

Since fiscal and monetary policies influence AD, real output, and the price levels, they can also impact the exchange rate as these are all factors of the supply and demand for a currency. For example, if a fiscal policy is put into place that cuts taxes, the AD and national output will shift right and increase, and the price level will rise. This means a higher demand for foreign goods and investments, an increase in supply, and depreciation of the country's currency.

Questions:

1. Assume that as a result of increased political instability, investors move their funds out of the country of Dion. How will this decision by investors affect the international value of Dion's currency on the foreign exchange market? Explain.

2. Under a flexible exchange-rate system, the Indian rupee will appreciate against the Japanese yen when

    (A) India's inflation rate exceeds Japan's
    (B) India has a trade deficit with Japan
    (C) Japan's economy enters a recession, but India's does not
    (D) Japan's money supply decreases while India's money supply increases
    (E) real interest rates in India increase relative to those in Japan

3. Assume that the real interest rates in both Canada and India have been 5 percent. Now the real interest rate in India increases to 8 percent. Using a correctly labeled graph of the foreign exchange market for the Canadian dollar, show the effect of the higher real interest rate in India on each of the following.

    (i) Supply of the Canadian dollar. Explain.
    (ii) The value of the Canadian dollar, assuming flexible exchange rates

Changes in the Foreign Exchange Market and Net Exports

Let's go back to our exchange rate graph of the British pound in comparison to the US dollar.

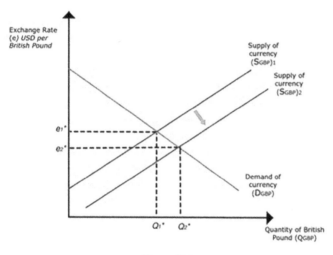

Figure 33.3

In this example, the supply of the British pound has increased, and the currency has depreciated. Meanwhile, in terms of the pound, the US dollar has appreciated. What happens to exports and imports? Any factor that changes the currency impacts net exports (X-M).

In Great Britain, American goods are now more expensive, as they need to supply more British pounds to buy dollars. In America, considering the dollar is now worth more than the British pound, UK goods are cheaper. The United States would now export fewer goods to the United Kingdom but import more from them. The United Kingdom imports fewer American goods and exports more of their own goods.

	Net Imports	Net Exports
CURRENCY DEPRECIATES	Decrease	Increase
CURRENCY APPRECIATES	Increase	Decrease

Module 34:
Real Interest Rates and International Capital Flows

Are international trade and exchange of currency the only things that can influence a country's domestic market? What about the flow of international capital?

The real interest rate is what determines if domestic assets are purchased by foreign buyers or if domestic buyers purchase foreign assets. Financial capital increases in a country with a higher interest rate and decreases in a country with a lower interest rate as investors are drawn to a higher rate due to a greater return.

When there is a difference of interest rates between two countries, this impacts the balance of payments, the exchange rate, and the market for loanable funds, which can directly affect the business cycles.

Example

Suppose you are in Texas and have American assets but see the interest rate rise in Brazil to a lot higher than the American rate. You decide to buy Brazilian financial assets—some Brazilian government bonds. What does this do?

- This will reduce the supply of loanable funds in the United States as the funds are now part of Brazil's market.
- It will increase the interest rate in the United States as the US market responds to a lower supply.
- The demand for Brazilian real (the Brazilian national currency) increases, since you will have to purchase the assets in Brazil's currency, causing the real to appreciate. The supply of the US dollars increases, since you need American dollars to purchase reals, and so the US dollar depreciates.

Central Bank Influence

Central banks can change the interest rate in the short run, which can change capital flow, exchange rates, and net exports. If an expansionary monetary policy is used in Canada, it will

- increase the Canadian money supply.
- decrease the Canadian interest rate.

In terms of the international market:

- A lower interest rate means lower demand for Canadian assets.
- Increase demand by Canadians for foreign assets, so increase the supply of the Canadian dollar
- Lower demand for Canadian currency, so the Canadian dollar will depreciate.

Module 1: Scarcity
Scarcity is defined as the condition where the limited supply of resources does not meet the wants and needs of consumers and it is the motivation behind economic choices. Almost all resources are limited and economic resources like labor, commodities, raw materials, and land become valuable because they are limited.

Module 2: Opportunity Cost and the Production Possibilities Curve
A trade-off occurs when a choice is made between two economic goods. The opportunity cost is simply what you lose when you do not choose an alternative. A good example of this would be the situation of a student choosing to take piano lessons on Saturdays instead of resting. The opportunity cost of Saturday lessons is the value of sleeping in on a Saturday. Know how to draw and label the production possibilities curve (PPC) which illustrates how production choices are made. Know how to explain shifts in the PPC and how to calculate the opportunity cost of two goods.

Module 3: Comparative Advantage and Gains from Trade
A comparative advantage exists when the opportunity cost of producing a good or service is lower than the opportunity cost of another country which produces the same good or service. The country with the comparative advantage in producing a good, should specialize in producing that good and trade it for other goods. Gains from trade arise when countries benefit from the economic trade of goods based on their specialization. Know how to define and find absolute advantage and comparative advantage, and how specialization occurs and can lead to gains from trade with two countries. Students often get confused here if they have not fully grasped the concept of opportunity cost and how to calculate it.

Module 4: Module 4: Demand
Demand refers to the relationship between a range of prices and the quantities of goods and services consumers would purchase, as shown in the demand curve and demand schedule. The demand curve is downward sloping reflecting the law of demand which

states that at higher prices, consumer demand less and vice versa. The law of diminishing marginal utility says that as consumption increases, the marginal utility derived from each additional unit declines. Know how to draw and explain the relationship between price and demand, and the factors that can shift the demand curve.

Module 5: Supply

Supply is defined as a supplier's willingness to produce an amount of goods and services at each price level. Know how to draw and explain the relationship between a range of prices and quantities supplied at those prices, and the factors that shift the supply curve. The supply curve is upward sloping – at higher prices, suppliers want to produce more in order to reap more revenues; while at lower prices, they will be willing to produce less, since revenue making opportunities decline.

Module 6: Market Equilibrium

Market Equilibrium is where the demand and supply curves meet, and it is the price and quantity of a good or service at which all economic actors are satisfied. Know how to graph and label the market and identify a surplus and shortage. Know how to explain the effect different factors have on shifts on supply and demand, and how equilibrium can be restored in the market.

Module 7: The Circular Flow Model

the circular flow model is an easy way to see how sectors of the economy interact within a closed economy. Money paid to the government from households is called leakage and mainly takes the form of taxes. Government spending pumps money back into the economy.

Module 8: Gross Domestic Product

GDP is calculated as: Consumption + Investment + Government Spending + Net Exports Any individual and household spending on goods and services is classified as consumption. Any business transactions are classified as investment spending in the calculation of GDP. Government spending includes large-scale federal government expenditure on roads and bridges, schools and hospitals, or city and municipal purchases of emergency flooding supplies and security etc.. Net exports: (Exports - Imports). Exports are sales of goods and services to foreign countries and add to GDP since it is money coming into the economy. Imports are purchases of goods and services from foreign countries and deduct from GDP since it means that money is leaving the country. Know how to calculate GDP, the limitations to GDP and the three ways of calculating GDP: the expenditure approach, the income approach and the production (or value added) approach.

Module 9: Unemployment

The unemployment rate refers to the percentage of unemployed workers in the total labor force despite being willing and able to work. The labor force of an economy is the total number of people who are both employed and unemployed. The remaining level of unemployment when an economy is healthy is called the natural rate of unemployment. Know how to define structural, frictional, cyclical and seasonal unemployment. Know how to calculate the unemployment rate, labor force and labor force participation rate. Also identify the limitations of using the unemployment rate. Remember that students, the elderly, the mentally and physically disabled are not included in the labor force and individuals who have not been looking for work for more than 6 months are considered discouraged workers, and also excluded from the labor force. Individuals who are willing and able to work full time but are only able to secure part time work, or work well below their qualification standards, are considered underemployed.

Module 10: Prices and Inflation

The consumer price index (CPI) is a common way governments measure inflation, which is the term used to describe an increase in prices. Know how to compute the CPI and the inflation rate, and identify the shortcomings of the CPI. Be able to explain how and why inflation can benefit borrowers and cause losses for lenders.

Module 11: Real vs. Nominal GDP

The nominal GDP as a measure of economic growth is flawed, because it has the tendency to overstate the growth of output since it does not take into consideration the changes in prices. Real GDP focuses on measuring the value of all final goods and services produced in an economy during a given year, considering the change in price levels from year to year. Know how to compute real GDP from nominal GDP.

Module 12: Business Cycle

The business cycle follows a wavelike pattern that shows the rise and fall in the production of goods and services in the economy and the economy's short-term movement in and out of recession. The business cycle experiences output gaps: the difference between the actual output and the potential output of an economy. Know the points on the business cycle graph like expansions, peaks, recessions and positive/negative output gaps.

Module 13: The Multiplier

The amount of each dollar that individuals generally spend is referred to as the marginal propensity to consume (MPC). In macro-economic theory, we assume that the remainder of each dollar earned that is not spent is saved, and that is called the marginal propensity to save (MPS).

The power of the multiplier effect is that initial spending provides ripple benefits throughout the economy. When, and only when new money is introduced into an economic system (let's say the government prints money in order to fund a new government project – the value of that money is felt long after the first transaction, but the value declines when money changes from one hand to the other since each person will save a percentage of it.

The expenditure multiplier quantifies the size of the change in aggregate demand that results from a change in any of the four components of aggregate demand. The tax multiplier causes a smaller change in GDP relative to the expenditure multiplier because people tend to save some of the tax cuts and pay tax increases by both less spending and saving less. Therefore the tax multiplier is smaller than the expenditure multiplier. Be able to explain the multiplier effect. Know the formulas for MPC, MPS and the spending multiplier.

Module 14: Aggregate Demand (AD)
Aggregate demand follows the same logic as the regular demand curve but refers to demand of an entire economy instead of an individual market. The AD curve illustrates the negative relationship between AD and real GDP. The negative slope of the AD curve is explained by the real wealth effect, the interest rate effect, and the exchange rate effect. Know how to graph the aggregate demand curve, identify the shifters of the aggregate demand curve and how they effect it on the graph.

Module 15: Aggregate Supply
Variable costs change depending on the level of a business's output, while fixed costs are costs companies face that do not change, no matter the level of output. There are no fixed costs in the long run; all costs are variable in the long run. The SRAS curve slopes upward due to sticky wages (input) and sticky prices (output). The long-run aggregate supply (LRAS) curve is vertical, suggesting that in the long term, output is fixed at a certain level, when all economic resources are used. Know how to graph the aggregate supply curves, identify the shifters of the aggregate supply curves and how they are effected on the graph.

Short-run equilibrium occurs when the aggregate demand and aggregate supply are equal. Long-run equilibrium occurs when the AD and SRAS curves intersect on the LRAS. An inflationary gap occurs when the short run equilibrium is to the right of the LRAS and causes a rise in wages while a recessionary gap occurs when the short run equilibrium is to the left of the LRAS and causes a fall in prices overall. Know to graph the short-run and long-run market equilibrium price levels and output levels. Know how to graph movements due to changes and shocks in the short and long run.

Module 16: Fiscal Policy
Fiscal policies are what government uses to fund itself and to achieve its objectives through government spending and tax/transfers. Governments use these policies to manage economic output, employment, and inflation rates. Changes in fiscal policy affect aggregate demand, GDP and price levels. Be able to define expansionary (aimed at increasing consumption) and contractionary (aimed at reducing consumption) policies, and automatic stabilizers. Know how to graph the short- run effects of a fiscal policy action on the AD-AS model.

Module 17: Financial Assets
The holder of a financial asset agrees to receive income as the buyer from the seller in the future. Know how to define loans, stocks, bonds and loan-backed securities. The rate of return or return on investment is the gain (or loss) on an investment, and financial risk occurs when the outcome of the value of an asset is unknown or there is uncertainty for the future. Liquidity refers to an asset's ability to be used right away; cash therefore is the most liquid asset. Know how to calculate the rate of return.

Module 18: Nominal vs Real Interest Rates
Interest is the cost of a loan. The real interest rate is adjusted for inflation and is the actual cost of borrowing, while the nominal rate is not adjusted for inflation. The expected inflation rate is used by banks in the absence of the ability to predict exactly what inflation will be. Know how to calculate the nominal and real interest rates.

Module 19: Definition, Measurement, and Functions of Money
Money has three main functions: medium of exchange, unit of account and store of value. The money-supplied measurements are M1 (includes cash, travelers checks, and checkable bank deposits) and M2 (includes M1 and near-moneys, or financial assets that cannot be directly used for payment, such as savings accounts). The monetary base (M0 or MB) includes currency in circulation and bank reserves. Know how to calculate M1, M2 and MB.

Module 20: Banking and the Expansion of the Money Supply
Balance sheets are what banks, other businesses, and even individuals use to summarize what they own of value and what they owe. Liabilities are the things you owe while assets are things you own. Banks are required to maintain a percentage of the money they receive in deposits to satisfy any deposit withdrawal which is called the required reserve ratio. Know how to draw and label a balance sheet, and the impact of the money multiplier.

Module 21: The Money Market
The money market is the supply and demand of highly liquid assets in a nation's economy. The demand for money is the relationship between the quantity of money (cash) people want to hold and the nominal interest rate. The supply of money is vertical as it does not depend on the interest rate because it is controlled by a nation's central bank. Know how to graph the money demand curve, money supply curve and the equilibrium in the money market. Certain factors can cause changes in the money demand: the price level, monetary policy, changes in GDP, and technology. Be able to identify the impacts these changes have and graph how the nominal interest rate adjusts to restore equilibrium.

Module 22: Monetary Policy
The central bank controls the supply of money in the money market through monetary policies. Expansionary or contractionary monetary policies are used to restore full employment. The three methods are: open- market operations, the required reserve ratio, and the discount rate. Know how to graph and explain the impact of any of the monetary policy actions on the money market model and the AD–AS model.

Module 23: The Loanable Funds Market
The loanable funds market shows the relationship between borrowers and savers in an economy. The demand of loanable funds curve shows the willingness to borrow money, and the supply of loanable funds curve shows the willingness to save money. Know how to graph the loanable funds market and the factors that change the supply and demand. Know how to calculate national savings in a closed and open economy.

Module 24: Fiscal and Monetary Policy Actions in the Short Run
Fiscal policy is made by the government and focuses on taxes and government spending, while monetary policy is made by the central bank and focuses on the supply of money, and they can be used together. Know how to graph and explain combined expansionary and contractionary policies. A policy lag is the time between when a problem arises in the economy and the effect of the policy actually starting to work. There are data, recognition, decision/legislative, implementation and effectiveness lags.

Module 25: The Phillips Curve
The Phillips curve shows the inverse relationship between inflation and unemployment. It is modeled by putting the rate of inflation on the vertical axis and the rate of unemployment on the horizontal axis. The short-run Phillips curve (SRPC) shows when there is high inflation, there is low unemployment while the long-run Phillips curve (LRPC) is vertical at the natural rate of unemployment. Know how to graph the Phillips curves and show

how it responds to changes in demand and supply. Know the three points the economy can be at on the curve: recession, equilibrium/full employment or inflationary gap.

Module 26: Money Growth and Inflation

Inflation results from increasing the money supply too quickly for a long period of time. The quantity theory of money states that any increase in the money supply causes an increase in the price level, when the velocity of money is fixed and output is at full employment output. The velocity of money (V) describes how many times a dollar circulates in the economy. Know the quantity theory of money equation and how to calculate supply, price and output.

Module 27: Government Deficits and the National Debt

The budget deficit is when spending and transfer payments exceed the government's tax revenue in a given year. The government must borrow that money and the accumulation of such debt is known as national or public debt. Know how to calculate government savings.

Module 28: Crowding Out

Crowding out is when a government borrows money at the expense of private-sector borrowing and investment, leading to less growth and less investment in the economy. Know how to graph the crowding out effect on the loanable funds market model. Long run crowding out can cause a lower rate of physical capital accumulation and eventually less economic growth.

Module 29: Economic Growth

To measure growth, we focus on GDP per capita over time and divide it by the population size. A single period of positive or negative GDP levels does not define economic growth as it could just be part of the natural business cycle so we look for long-term trends when discussing growth. Improvements in technology, human capital and physical capital can shift the PPC outwards. Know the aggregate production function, which shows how productivity in terms of output per worker relies on the amount of physical capital and human capital as well as the state of technology.

Module 30: Public Policy and Economic Growth

Policies aimed at improving productivity focus on the labor supply and in turn increase GDP per capita and economic growth. Policies can increase economic growth by investing in technology and capital, which push the PPC as there is more capacity to produce. Supply-side fiscal policies affect AD, AS, and potential output in the short and long run.

Module 31: Balance of Payments Accounts
The current account records transactions of merchandise, services, interest, and dividend income between one country and the rest of the world. The capital and financial account records financial capital transfers and purchases or sales of assets between countries. A surplus in the capital and financial account means there has been a net inflow of financial capital, while a deficit means there has been a net outflow of financial capital. The balance of payments is an accounting system that records a country's international transactions. The current account and the capital and financial account make up the balance of payments. Know how to calculate CA, CFA and BOP.

Module 32: Exchange Rates
An exchange rate is the value of a country's currency in terms of the currency of another country. The demand and supply of a currency impacts that currency's exchange rate or relative value of one country's currency to another. A nation's currency can either appreciate or depreciate. Know how to calculate an exchange rate and define the determinants that can shift the supply and demand of a currency.

Module 33: The Foreign Exchange Market
Just as we trade stocks and bonds on the stock market, we can trade currencies on a global decentralized market called the foreign exchange market. Know how to graph the foreign exchange market and identify the equilibrium exchange rate.

Module 34: Effect of Changes in Policies and Economic Conditions on the Foreign Exchange Market
Changes in the supply and demand of a currency cause it to appreciate or depreciate in a flexible exchange regime. Factors that change the demand of a currency are preferences, interest rates, expected future exchange rates, price levels and the national income. Factors that influence the supply of a currency are based on the demand of another currency. Know how to graph and show the determinants of the supply and demand of a currency. Since fiscal and monetary policies influence AD, real output, and the price levels, they can also impact the exchange rate as these are all factors of the supply and demand for a currency.

Module 35: Changes in the Foreign Exchange Market and Net Exports
Any factor that changes the currency impacts net exports (X-M). Know how to graph what happens to the value of a nation's currency and their imports and exports.

Module 36: Real Interest Rates and International Capital Flows
The real interest rate is what determines if domestic assets are purchased by foreign buyers or if domestic buyers purchase foreign assets. When there is a difference

of interest rates between two countries, this impacts the balance of payments, the exchange rate, and the market for loanable funds, which can directly affect the business cycles. Know how to graph these changes. The central bank can also use monetary policy to change the domestic interest rate in the short run, which will affect net capital inflows.

Answers

Module 2

1. (i) One point for a correctly labeled PPC
    (ii) One point for labeling points C and D and for showing a movement toward the curve and an increase in military goods

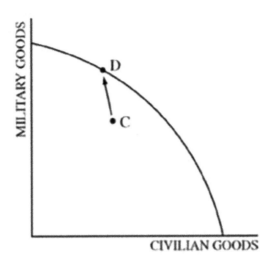

2. C
3. A
4. (i) One point for a correctly labeled PPC for Sweden with food on the horizontal axis, capital goods on the vertical axis, and the relevant numerical values plotted
    (ii) 3 points:

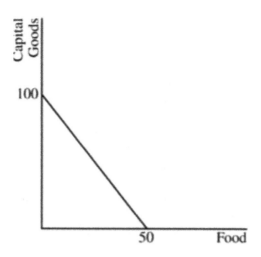

- One point for showing point I inside the PPC
- One point for showing E on the PPC
- One point for U outside the PPC

Module 3

1.   D
2.   (i) One point for stating that John has the absolute advantage in producing donuts and can produce more donuts than Erica in one day (200 > 150)
(ii) One point for stating that Erica has a comparative advantage in producing donuts, and her opportunity cost of producing one donut (1/3 of a cupcake) is less than John's opportunity cost of producing one donut (1/2 of a cupcake).
(iii) 2 points:
- One point for indicating that John will benefit from specialization and trade.
- One point for indicating that Erica will not benefit from specialization and trade.

Module 5

1.   D

Module 6

1.   C

Module 7

1.   C

Module 9

1. C
2. D
3. D
4. (i) One point for correctly calculating the unemployment rate as 10 percent ($20,000/200,000 \times 100 = 10\%$)
   (ii) One point for correctly calculating the labor force participation rate as 66.67 percent ($200,000/300,000 \times 100 = 66.67\%$)
5. One point for stating that the natural rate of unemployment will not change in the long run

Module 10

1. (i) One point for calculating the inflation rate as 10 percent ($= 5/50$).
   (ii) One point for stating that the real wage will be lower
2. B
3. E
4. D

Module 11

1. (i) One point for calculating the nominal GDP for 2010 as $145 ($= 20 + 100 + 25$).
   (ii) One point for calculating the real GDP in 2010 as $100 ($= 20 + 60 + 20$).
2. A
3. D

Module 12

1. C

Module 13

1. A
2. D
3. B
4. One point for calculating the maximum change in real GDP: Change in GDP = $(1/0.25) \times \$100$ billion $= \$400$ billion
5. (i) One point for correctly calculating the minimum change in government spending required to change aggregate demand by the amount of the output gap as an increase of $8 billion ($= \$40$ billion/5).

(ii) One point for correctly calculating the minimum change in taxes required to change aggregate demand by the amount of the output gap as a decrease of $10 billion ($40 billion/4).

Module 14

1. One point for stating that Argentina's AD will fall because the purchase results in increased imports or decreased net exports, which are components of aggregate demand.
2. D
3. A
4. B
5. (i) One point for stating that US exports will decrease and the fall in income in the Euro zone reduces the demand for US goods.

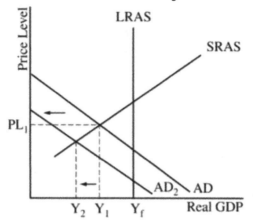

(ii) One point for showing a leftward shift of the AD curve and US real output on the graph.

(iii) One point for stating that unemployment in the United States will increase.

Module 15

6. C
7. E
8. D
9. E

(Changes to the AD-AS Model in the Short Run)

10. E
11. A
12. A

Module 15

1. (i) 2 points:
    - One point for stating that AD increases
    - One point for explaining that the decrease in taxes raises disposable income and increases consumption spending.
    (ii) 2 points:

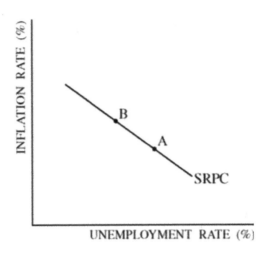

    - One point for a correctly labeled graph of the Phillips curve
    - One point for the correct initial and current positions
2. B
3. B
4. C

Module 16

1. D
2. One point for the correct calculation of the real interest rate: 8% - 6% = 2%.
3. (i) One point for stating that the nominal interest rate will increase
    (ii) One point for stating that the real interest rate will remain unchanged
4. One point for calculating the real interest rate: 8% - 3% = 5%

Module 18

1. D
2. B
3. A
4. D

Module 19

1. (i) One point for determining the total change in reserves: $50 million.
   (ii) One point for calculating the maximum possible change in the money supply: $10 \times \$50 = \$500$ million.
2. One point for stating that bank loans will decrease.
3. B
4. E
5. E
6. One point for stating that the Federal Reserve purchase will not initially affect commercial banks' required reserves.
7. One point for defining the discount rate as the interest rate the Federal Reserve charges banks for borrowing money from its discount window

Module 20

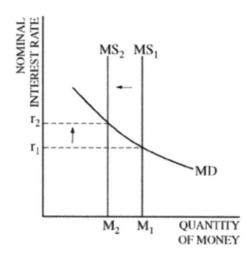

1. - One point for correctly labelled graph of the money market.
   - One point for showing leftward shift of the money supply curve and an increase in the nominal interest rate.
2. B

Module 21

1. D
2. C
3. E
4. E

5. (i) One point for identifying the buying of bonds as the correct open-market operation.
   (ii) 2 points:

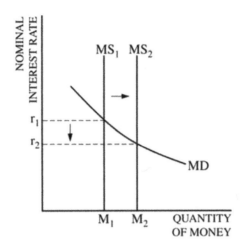

- One point for drawing a correctly labeled graph of the money market
- One point for showing a rightward shift of the money supply curve, resulting in a lower interest rate.
(iii) 2 points:
- One point for stating that the real interest rate will fall
- One point for explaining that with the price level remaining constant, when the nominal interest rate falls, the real interest rate also falls
(iv) One point for stating that the real GDP will increase in the short run and that investment or consumption increases, causing aggregate demand to increase

6. C

Module 22

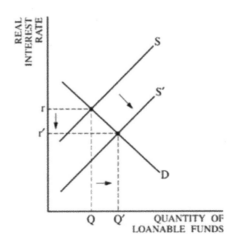

1.   (i) One point for drawing a correctly labeled graph of the loanable funds market and showing a rightward shift of the supply curve and the change in the real interest rate.

(ii) 2 points:

- One point for stating that the decrease in the real interest rate caused interest-sensitive spending to increase

- One point for stating that the increase in aggregate demand increases output, which causes an increase in employment

2.   2 points:

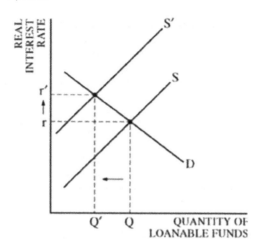

3.

- One point for a correctly labeled graph of the loanable funds market. The graph must have correctly labeled axes and supply and demand curves.

- One point for showing a leftward shift of the supply curve and a higher interest rate.

Module 23

1.   E
2.   A
3.   B
4.   D

Module 24

1.   2 points:

- One point for stating that the short-run AS curve will shift to the right in the long run and that nominal wages will fall in response to high unemployment.

- One point for stating that LRPC will remain unchanged

Module 26

1. C
2. B
3. E

Module 28

1. One point is earned for stating that a higher interest rate will result in a decrease in the rate of economic growth. One point is earned for explaining that the interest rate increase reduces investment, which causes a decline in the rate of growth of the capital stock.
2. C

Module 29

1.

(i) One point is earned for stating that investment spending will decrease.
(ii) One point is earned for explaining that the decrease in investment slows down capital formation, leading to a reduction in the economic growth rate.
2. C

Module 30

1. One point is earned for stating that the United States current account will be in surplus or increases because exports are recorded as a credit in the current account.
2. B
3. A
4. One point is earned for stating that the U.S. current account will be in deficit and for explaining that an increase in the U.S. real GDP increases the U.S.'s demand for European goods and services, which increases imports.

Module 31

1. (i) One point is earned for stating that aggregate demand in Singapore will increase and for explaining that the depreciating Singaporean dollar increases Singapore's exports to European Union countries because the price of those exports — in terms of euros — decreases.

(ii) One point is earned for stating that employment in Singapore will increase because Singapore's real GDP increases and it takes more labor to produce more goods and services.

Module 32

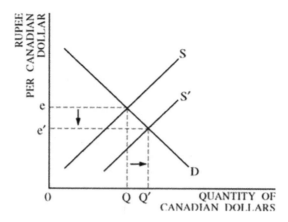

1. One point is earned for the correctly labeled graph of the foreign exchange market.

   One point is earned for showing that the supply of Canadian dollars will increase, or the supply curve will shift to the right.

   One point is earned for explaining that Canadian investors will be attracted by the higher real interest rate in India and increase their purchase of Indian financial assets.

   One point is earned for showing that the Canadian dollar depreciates against the Indian rupee.

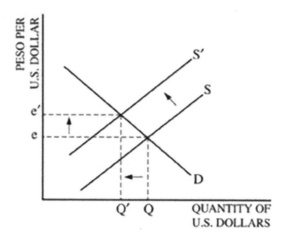

One point is earned for a correctly labeled graph of the dollar market.

One point is earned for showing a leftward shift of the supply curve and indicating that the value of the dollar against the peso increases, using arrows, labels or dotted lines.

2.   A
3.   D

Module 33

1.   One point is earned for stating that Dion's currency will depreciate. One point is earned for explaining that capital flight increases the supply of and/or decreases the demand for Dion's currency in the foreign exchange market, thereby lowering the market equilibrium exchange rate.
2.   E

Reference:
Exam questions are from past AP Macroeconomics exams published by the College Board.

CPSIA information can be obtained
at www.ICGtesting.com
Printed in the USA
LVHW071530060921
697128LV00014B/1516